GREAT MYSTERIES

The
Assassination of
President Kennedy

OPPOSING VIEWPOINTS®

Look for these and other exciting *Great Mysteries: Opposing Viewpoints* books:

GREAT MYSTERIES

The Assassination of President Kennedy

OPPOSING VIEWPOINTS®

by Jeffrey Waggoner

Greenhaven Press, Inc.   P.O. Box 289009, San Diego, California 92128-9009

Library of Congress Cataloging-in-Publication Data

Waggoner, Jeffrey, 1960-
    The assassination of President Kennedy : opposing viewpoints / by Jeffrey Waggoner.
        p.   cm. — (Great mysteries)
    Includes bibliographical references.
    Summary: Examines the conflicting evidence into the search for the killer of President John F. Kennedy.
    ISBN 0-89908-068-5
    1. Kennedy, John F. (John Fitzgerald), 1917-1963—Assassination—Juvenile literature. [1. Kennedy, John F. (John Fitzgerald), 1917-1963—Assassination.]   I. Title. II. Series: Great mysteries (Saint Paul, Minn.)
E842.9.W26   1989
364. 1'524—dc20   89-37442
                                                CIP
                                                AC

"When men and women lose the sense of mystery, life will prove to be a gray and dreary business, only with difficulty to be endured."

Harold T. Wilkins, *author of* Strange Mysteries of Time and Space

Contents

Introduction

This book is written for the curious—those who want to explore the mysteries that are everywhere. To be human is to be constantly surrounded by wonderment. How do birds fly? Are ghosts real? Can animals and people communicate? Was King Arthur a real person or a myth? Why did Amelia Earhart disappear? Did history really happen the way we think it did? Where did the world come from? Where is it going?

Great Mysteries: Opposing Viewpoints books are intended to offer the reader an opportunity to explore some of the many mysteries that both trouble and intrigue us. For the span of each book, we want the reader to feel that he or she is a scientist investigating the extinction of the dinosaurs, an archaeologist searching for clues to the origin of the great Egyptian pyramids, a psychic detective testing the existence of ESP.

One thing all mysteries have in common is that there is no ready answer. Often there are *many* answers but none on which even the majority of authorities agrees. *Great Mysteries: Opposing Viewpoints* books introduce the intriguing views of the experts, allowing the reader to participate in their explorations, their theories, and their disagreements as they try to explain the mysteries of our world.

But most readers won't want to stop here. These *Great Mysteries: Opposing Viewpoints* aim to stimulate the reader's curiosity. Although truth is often impossible to discover, the search is fascinating. It is up to the reader to examine the evidence, to decide whether the answer is there—or to explore further.

"Penetrating so many secrets, we cease to believe in the unknowable. But there it sits nevertheless, calmly licking its chops."

H.L. Mencken, American essayist

One

Who Would Have Killed President Kennedy, and Why?

On Friday, November 22, 1963, just southwest of the intersection of Elm and Houston streets in Dallas, Texas, hundreds of people witnessed one of the most famous murders in recent history. The victim was the president of the United States. The assassination lasted between six and eight seconds. But by the time those few seconds were over, John Fitzgerald Kennedy, the thirty-fifth president of the United States, had received two gunshot wounds. One of them was fatal. The first shot hit Kennedy in the region of his lower neck or upper back. Doctors said he could have survived this first wound if he had sustained no others. The second, though, was fatal. It caused massive damage to Kennedy's skull and brain.

Some witnesses stood only a few feet away from the president when the shots rang out at 12:30 that afternoon. Hundreds of others watched from farther away as Kennedy rode past them in an uncovered limousine on an otherwise average Friday afternoon in the South.

At 7:08 that morning, Dallas Police Chief Jesse Curry reminded the city that the president would arrive in just a few hours. Law enforcement officials

President Kennedy's open convertible moved through downtown Dallas, passing crowds of people, just minutes before he was murdered.

John F. Kennedy is sworn into office while President Eisenhower and Mrs. Kennedy look on. He was immensely popular with Americans at the time.

were particularly worried that Kennedy faced potential danger in Dallas. In a televised announcement, Chief Curry warned that anyone who tried to disrupt Kennedy's visit would face immediate police response. He hoped to avoid trouble before it happened.

Police departments are always concerned when an important person visits. But the Dallas Police Department had reason to be more concerned than usual about Kennedy's visit to Dallas: Many Americans were intensely dissatisfied with Kennedy's presidency. Some of his most outspoken opponents lived in the South; many of them lived in Dallas.

Early in his presidential term, Kennedy enjoyed an unusually high popularity with American voters. In April 1961, just three months after taking office, public opinion polls showed that 83 percent of all Americans approved of his performance as president. By the summer and fall of 1963, however, his popularity had dropped sharply; in November 1963, less than 60 percent of American voters supported him.

Kennedy's term was due to end in 1964, and he planned to run for re-election. In late 1963, he already was thinking about winning votes for the upcoming election. He and his advisors thought a goodwill trip would improve his popularity throughout the South. Opposition to Kennedy's policies was strong there, but that was precisely why, politically, the trip was necessary.

Liberal vs. Conservative

Most of Kennedy's problems with Southern voters stemmed from his relatively "liberal" policies on key issues affecting the nation. The world *liberal* comes from a Latin word that means *free* or *to be free from*. An important word in American history, *liberty*, derives from the same source. When we say that Kennedy was a liberal politician, then, we mean that he was "free" from traditional ways of solving the nation's problems. He was willing to try new, different solutions to old problems.

Kennedy's new programs were not always successful. What angered more conservative citizens the most, however, was not that his policies did not work. It was the fact that he was willing—and even eager—to change. In general, we say conservatives prefer to "conserve," or "save," the traditions and ways they already know. To many of Kennedy's staunchest opponents, observing traditional ways of solving problems was more important than looking for new, perhaps better, solutions.

Kennedy and Civil Rights

One of the areas in which Kennedy sought change was civil rights. At the time, many white citizens in the South treated nonwhite citizens as inferiors; it was traditional in the South to treat white people and black people differently. Blacks, for instance, were forbidden by law to drink from the same water fountains from which whites drank. According to the law, blacks were second-class citizens in the South.

Two hundred thousand people marched on August 28, 1963 in Washington, DC demanding equal rights. Here Martin Luther King Jr. delivered his "I have a dream" speech.

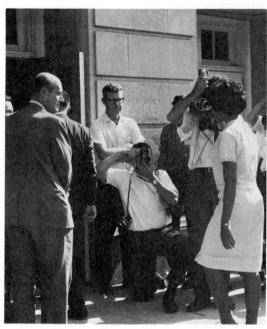

Governor George Wallace confronts Deputy Attorney General Nicholas Katzenbach at the University of Alabama when two black students attempted to enroll for classes.

Kennedy wanted to solve the problem of interracial relations another way: He wanted all races to be treated the same. Earlier in 1963, in June, he had openly supported the right of all minorities to attend any American university for which they were qualified.

Until June 1963, no black had ever enrolled for classes at the University of Alabama. That month George Wallace, the governor of Alabama, stood in the university's doorway to physically bar two black students from enrolling.

Kennedy reacted by sending the Deputy Attorney General of the United States, Nicholas Katzenbach, to Alabama. Katzenbach would personally escort the two students into the university. Kennedy also "federalized" a division of National Guard troops and sent them to the university. The troops' presence discouraged violence against Katzenbach and the two students.

A full-scale riot was possible, but the situation ended peacefully. The two black students enrolled in the University of Alabama. Kennedy had won one episode in the emerging civil rights debate. In the process, though, he had deeply angered supporters of racial division.

Kennedy's stand on civil rights caused only part of the concern for his safety expressed by the Dallas police that Friday morning. Unfavorable reactions to his policies on other issues disturbed them even more.

Kennedy and Cuba

American relations with Cuba was an issue which was particularly important for Southern citizens. Cuba is located only ninety miles off the coast of Florida. Any Cuban aggression against the United States probably would begin somewhere in the South. Cuba had undergone a political revolution in 1959. Its new leader, Fidel Castro, eagerly established ties with the Soviet Union soon after he assumed power.

For America, the prospect of Cuba becoming a Soviet base of operations was intolerable. From the earliest days of his presidency, relations between Kennedy and Cuban leaders were strained. Those relations became even more strained in April 1961 when a group of American-trained Cuban guerrillas failed in an attempted counterrevolution against Castro's new government. Their failed invasion took place at the Cuban port called the Bay of Pigs.

At a crucial point, sending in American military support might have turned the invasion in the guerrillas' favor. But Kennedy refused to let American forces participate. Plans for the invasion were not his; the Bay of Pigs invasion was a leftover project from the previous administration of President Dwight D. Eisenhower. Kennedy never liked the idea and could not support it wholeheartedly.

Some Americans thought Kennedy's refusal had left the anti-Castro Cubans to die for nothing on the Cuban coast. Members of the CIA (the Central Intelligence Agency) who had trained the guerrillas

''Lee Harvey Oswald was a partisan of Fidel Castro, and an admitted Marxist. . . . But for Castro and the Bay of Pigs disaster there would have been no Fair Play for Cuba Committee. And perhaps no assassin named Lee Harvey Oswald.''

CIA employee E. Howard Hunt, *Give Us This Day.*

''The committee believes, on the basis of the evidence available to it, that the Cuban government was not involved in the assassination of President Kennedy.''

Report of the Select Committee on Assassinations, U.S. House of Representatives, July 1979.

The president delivered a report to the country on November 2, 1962 telling Americans that the Soviet missile bases in Cuba were being destroyed and that U.S. surveillance would continue.

Map of Cuba which shows the location of the Bay of Pigs and its proximity to the United States.

reacted bitterly; they felt that President Kennedy had betrayed their mission. Families of the Cuban guerrillas also thought Kennedy had betrayed their sons by not sending in American troops when it became obvious that the guerrillas were badly outnumbered.

Relations with both Cuba and the Soviet Union worsened in 1962 during a tense thirteen-day episode known as the Cuban Missile Crisis. In October 1962, American aerial surveillance detected offensive nuclear missiles on Cuba. The missiles belonged to the Soviet Union.

On October 22, President Kennedy made a dramatic television address. He demanded that Soviet premier Nikita Khrushchev immediately remove all the missiles and cease all military activities in Cuba. He established a naval and air blockade to prevent more Soviet weapons from entering Cuba. He said that America was prepared to respond harshly if the Soviets did not remove their weapons from Cuban soil.

The world waited anxiously for Khrushchev's reply. Six tense days later, the premier responded: The

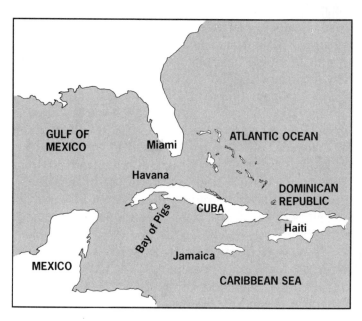

Fidel Castro and Nikita Khrushchev show their support for each other at the United Nations.

Soviet Union would stop its Cuban missile operations. In return, Khrushchev wanted America to agree not to invade Cuba again and to lift its marine and aerial blockade of the island. Kennedy agreed.

Kennedy had won another important victory, this time against foreign aggression. But just as his civil rights victory cost him support, so did the Cuban Missile Crisis.

Some groups, like the John Birch Society and the Minutemen, thought that Kennedy should have acted more forcefully against both the Soviet Union and Cuba. They thought he should not have promised to keep American troops out of Cuba. In fact, they even wanted the United States to openly participate in removing Fidel Castro from office. Groups like these disagreed with Kennedy's Cuban policies strongly enough to want him out of office.

John Kennedy confers with brother Robert at the White House.

Kennedy and Organized Crime

Other Kennedy policies caused problems for him, too. From the outset of his short administration, Kennedy and his brother, U.S. Attorney General Robert F. Kennedy, made stopping organized crime a top priority. No presidential administration in history had taken cleaning up organized crime as seriously as did the Kennedy administration. By 1963, it was clear that the Kennedys were winning their war on the nation's underworld.

Robert Kennedy was famous for the zeal with which he prosecuted criminals. He applied his eagerness to the Justice Department, over which the attorney general has control. In less than three years, Robert Kennedy quadrupled the size of entire sections of the Justice Department. His expansions made the department more effective at gathering crucial evidence for federal prosecutors to use in court.

As a result, arrested criminals were convicted more often with Robert Kennedy as attorney general. Convictions on racketeering charges, for example, more than quadrupled between 1961, the year the Kennedy administration began, and November 1963. Such dramatic increases were a direct result of Robert Kennedy's spirited persistence and the full support he enjoyed from his brother, the president.

In fact, the Kennedys' campaign against crime was so successful that the Mafia—the worldwide network of organized crime—wanted at least one Kennedy, preferably the attorney general, dead. Law enforcement agencies (and even a few private citizens) knew this before the assassination. The Kennedy name regularly surfaced in backroom Mafia discussions. In 1962, for instance, FBI surveillance overheard Willie Weisberg, a Philadelphia thug, making this remark to Philadelphia Mafia boss Angelo Bruno:

> With [President] Kennedy, a guy should take a knife . . . and stab and kill the [obscenity]. . . . Somebody should kill the [obscenity]. . . . I hope I get a week's notice. I'll kill. Right in the [obscenity] White House. Somebody's got to get rid of this [obscenity].

Remarks like these, savage though they are, were routine for Mafia members between January 1961 and November 1963. Both Kennedys dedicated large portions of their public lives to ridding American society of its criminals. In the process, some of the nation's most experienced murderers developed a fierce hatred for the Kennedys. In 1963, certain members of the Mafia unquestionably hated President Kennedy enough to take his life.

Many Potential Assassins

The Mafia, southern conservative extremists, and CIA operatives and anti-Castro Cubans still bitter over the failed Bay of Pigs invasion—all three groups had sufficient motive in November 1963 to kill John Ken-

Angelo Bruno is being held in a Dallas jail for federal agents who want to deport him for his illegal Mafia activities.

"The Commission has concluded that the shots which killed President Kennedy and wounded Governor Connally were fired from the sixth floor window at the southeast corner of the Texas School Book Depository Building."

Warren Commission Report, September 27, 1964.

"Sixty-four known witnesses indicated that shots originated from forward of the motorcade, from the vicinity of the Grassy Knoll, lending further credence to the physical evidence that President Kennedy was hit from the right front."

Writers David S. Lifton and David Welsh, *Ramparts*.

nedy. Another suspect was the Cuban government. It had learned earlier in the fall of 1963 of CIA assassination plots against Cuban premier Castro. Some interpreted Castro's own comments about the plots as hints that Cuba would retaliate against the American head of state. As always, another possible suspect was the single gunman, acting alone, who would kill a president for no other reason than to put his own name into history books.

Kennedy's brief presidency angered many groups of people, so one can find potential assassins in many directions. In the years since the assassination, though, three possibilities—the lone assassin, the Mafia, and the CIA—have received the most investigative attention.

Bedlam in Dealey Plaza

Investigators could have looked in many places for many suspects after the murder that Friday afternoon. But within eight minutes of the assassination, one line of evidence attracted more attention than any other.

Some witnesses reported having seen a rifle barrel extending outside a sixth-floor window of the Texas School Book Depository building at the corner of Elm and Houston streets. Dallas motorcycle policeman Marrion L. Baker even noticed pigeons flying from the top of the depository, as if they were startled, just seconds after the shooting.

On the sixth floor of the depository, police found three empty rifle shells below one corner window. In another corner they found a 6.5 mm Italian-made rifle. When they learned later that night that the rifle was owned by a depository employee—Lee Harvey Oswald—the search for Kennedy's assassin seemed to have narrowed quickly.

Investigators turned up other evidence that day, though, which suggested that a gunman had fired on the president from south of the depository. Witnesses who were closest to Kennedy at the time thought at least one shot had come from the north side of Elm Street, about one hundred yards south of the depository. A few people even reported seeing a puff of smoke rise from a line of trees to the right of the street on which Kennedy's limousine was traveling.

One couple who stood on the north curb of Elm thought they and their children were directly in the line of the gunman's fire. They pushed their children to the ground and dove on top of them to protect them. A motorcycle policeman who rode near the left rear bumper of the presidential limousine saw pieces of Kennedy's skull fly loose and fall to the left. If the

This photo of the Texas School Book Depository was marked for the Warren Commission by a witness who sat on the retaining wall at the corner of Elm and Houston to watch the motorcade. Window A indicates the spot where he saw a man with a rifle. Window B is where he saw people on the fifth floor watching the parade.

This inside view of the window from which Kennedy's assassin fired is inspected by police officers and reporters on November 22.

fatal shot had struck from behind, from the Texas School Book Depository, then the impact of the bullet should have thrown fragments of Kennedy's skull *forward*. According to such witnesses, at least one shot—probably the fatal one—had to have come from Kennedy's right.

Was it possible that the rifle and empty shells found in the depository were fakes? Could the assassin (or assassins) have planted the evidence to make Lee Harvey Oswald look like the president's killer?

Suspects and Witnesses, but No Answers

Serious questions about the assassination persist even today. Who killed President Kennedy, and why? No solid, certain answers have surfaced.

Of the hundreds of witnesses who lined Elm and Houston streets that day, more than twenty carried photographic equipment. Most of these people were taking still photos of the motorcade. A few others were using home movie cameras. So many cameras were in use during the assassination that it has been called "the most photographed murder in history."

Police routinely solve *un*witnessed murders. With so many witnesses and photographs, solving this case should have been easy. At the time, it was fair to expect a satisfactory explanation soon.

But to this day, we still have not found that explanation. The mystery of John F. Kennedy's assassination has only grown with time. One investigator, Josiah Thompson, has commented that this might be the strangest aspect of the entire perplexing case. Most murders eventually narrow down to one clear explanation that most reasonable people can accept as the truth. Just the opposite has happened with the Kennedy investigation. Instead of making the picture clearer, each new piece of evidence, each new interpretation of existing evidence, only seems to blur the picture further.

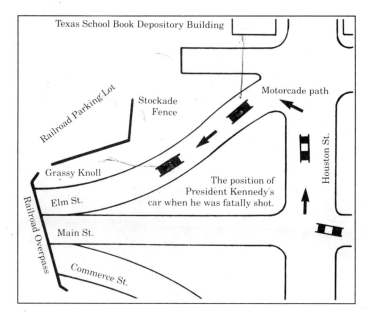

This diagram gives an overhead view of the area of the assassination. Note the Depository building, the grassy knoll, and the position of the president's car.

Contradiction and mystery have plagued the case from the very beginning. Many witnesses, most early newspaper accounts, and all the Dallas doctors said the fatal head shot struck Kennedy's right temple. The official autopsy report, however, stated that it entered at the base of Kennedy's skull, from behind.

The air of mystery also includes the people directly involved in the case. On Sunday, November 24, 1963, two days after the assassination, Lee Harvey Oswald, the prime suspect, was killed on national television by Dallas nightclub owner Jack Ruby. Before Oswald was killed, he told police more than once that he was not guilty, that he was ''just a patsy.'' He could have been lying—or he could have been hinting at a larger truth in the case, a conspiracy. Oswald's killer, Ruby, was known to have direct ties to organized crime. Was it possible that Jack Ruby, acting on someone else's orders, killed Lee Harvey Oswald in order to silence him?

Seconds after the assassin fired his shots, photographer James Altgens took this picture. The president's left arm has just jerked up and Mrs. Kennedy's gloved hand is reaching out to him. Behind the tree is the School Book Depository.

That question and others about John F. Kennedy's assassination have disturbed America ever since that weekend in Dallas in 1963. No theory yet satisfactorily explains every aspect of the case. We know the most important details. There have been formal and informal, public and private inquiries into those details. And yet, today, all we know for certain is that a promising world leader died as a result of what happened that day in Dallas. Explaining exactly how and why John F. Kennedy died is perhaps more difficult today than it was on Friday, November 22, 1963.

''The shots which killed President Kennedy and wounded Governor Connally were fired by Lee Harvey Oswald.''

Warren Commission Report, September 27, 1964.

''The president was killed by a person or persons unknown.''

Reporter George O'Toole, *Penthouse*.

A polaroid photo taken by a bystander records the instant the bullet strikes President Kennedy's head. The fatally wounded president slumps against his wife.

Two

One Assassin, Acting Alone— The "Official" Theory

Taken in April of 1963 in his Dallas backyard, this photo of Lee Harvey Oswald shows him holding what may have been the gun used to shoot John Kennedy. Note that he is also wearing a revolver and holding a newspaper called *The Militant*.

Doctors at Dallas's Parkland Hospital pronounced President Kennedy dead at 1:00 that afternoon. Almost two hours later, at 2:48, Vice President Lyndon B. Johnson was sworn in aboard Air Force One as the nation's new chief executive.

One week later, President Johnson created the President's Commission on the Assassination of President Kennedy. He appointed Earl Warren, chief justice of the United States Supreme Court, to head the commission. Six other public officials—four congressmen, a former director of the CIA, and an influential New York City attorney—served on the commission. Because Warren directed its activities, the commission was known simply as the Warren Commission.

In September 1964, just ten months after its creation, the Warren Commission issued its report on the assassination. The Warren Report appeared to be an exhaustive, thorough inquiry into Kennedy's death. The published report was more than 800 pages long. The commission and its staff had heard testimony from 489 people who were or might have been involved with the assassination. An additional twenty-six volumes of "Hearings and Exhibits" accompanied

The Warren Commission from left: Rep. Gerald Ford, Rep. Hale Boggs, Senator Richard Russell, Chief Justice Earl Warren, Senator John Sherman Cooper, New York banker John J. McCloy, former CIA director Allen Dulles, and J. Leo Rankin, the commission's general counsel.

the report for anyone interested enough to examine the commission's research.

The Warren Commission's most significant conclusion was that one man, Lee Harvey Oswald, acted alone and pulled the trigger behind every shot fired in Dealey Plaza on November 22, 1963. Circumstantial evidence gathered just after the assassination supported that conclusion. After examining peripheral evidence and Oswald's background, the commission was satisfied that its conclusion was correct.

Who Was Lee Harvey Oswald?

Although Lee Harvey Oswald lived only one month past his twenty-fourth birthday, his biography contains an unusually large number of unexplained gaps. On many occasions, his whereabouts were simply unknown. At other times, when researchers do know where he was, they can only speculate about why he might have been at a given place at a given time.

He was known to disappear for days, sometimes weeks, at a time. He was seen accepting a package from a known agent of the FBI. He defected from the United States to live in the Soviet Union, threatening to turn over military secrets to Soviet authorities as he entered their country. And yet, two-and-a-half years after his defection, the U.S. State Department loaned this former defector and possible traitor the money he needed for the trip home. Why would the U.S. State Department go out of its way to help Oswald, an apparently insignificant citizen whose recent actions amounted to treason?

Oddities like these occurred frequently over the last six to seven years of Oswald's life. Almost all of them remain unexplained.

Oswald's Early Life

The world into which Lee Oswald was born in New Orleans in 1939 was unstable and poor. His mother, Marguerite, had seen her first marriage end in divorce. Two months before Lee was born, Mrs. Oswald's second husband—Lee's father—died. That left Marguerite Oswald to support two young boys, Lee and his older brother Robert, on the low wages most women earned in the 1940s and 1950s. She was willing to move her family often if moving meant a chance to make more money. She moved her family to Dallas after her third marriage. When that marriage failed, she and her two youngest boys moved to New York. After Robert joined the Marine Corps, Lee and his mother moved again, this time back to New Orleans.

As a boy, Oswald showed an active, curious intelligence and a relatively high IQ of 118. He loved to read, but he quickly lost interest in formal education. By the time he was twelve, he had developed a problem with truancy.

The turning point in Oswald's life occurred in 1954. That was the year that two Americans, Julius

"As we pored over the thousands of pages of FBI and Secret Service reports and raised questions, it soon appeared that Oswald had to be involved in the assassination itself."

Warren Commission lawyer David W. Belin, *November 22, 1963: You Are the Jury*.

"All sorts of evidence was immediately seized that strongly implicated Oswald—but there is not a single piece of it that cannot be reasonably and rationally challenged."

Author Henry Hurt, *Reasonable Doubt*.

and Ethel Rosenberg, were arrested and tried for treason for selling secrets of atomic bomb construction to the Soviet Union. One day, purely by chance, a woman who was protesting in favor of the Rosenbergs handed young Oswald a pamphlet. It defended the Rosenbergs, and it also spurred Oswald's interest in Marxism, the social and economic philosophy adopted by the Soviet Union.

Marxism was founded by a German philosopher, Karl Marx, in the mid-nineteenth century. Marx thought "capitalistic" economies—like that of the United States—were doomed to failure. He thought they were based on greed and cruel exploitation of the people who perform the labor in any business. According to Marx, in such economies business owners always profit more than their workers. He predicted that an economy based on private ownership would eventually collapse; working-class resentment of owners would become strong enough to cause a revolution. Marx wanted to remove the profit incentive by having a nation's government own all property. That way, he theorized, a nation would exist for the common good of all its citizens. In Marx's

Ethel and Julius Rosenberg are being transported to prison after being convicted of espionage. Their conviction and death sentence aroused passionate responses from socialists around the world.

ideal world, divisions between social classes would be abolished. There would be no rich and no poor. No one would own property, so, theoretically, all would share the benefits of property equally.

Such ideas immediately appealed to the fifteen-year-old Oswald. He knew his mother worked long, difficult hours. No matter how hard she worked, though, she and her family continued to live in poverty. Someone, Oswald must have thought, was profiting from his mother's labors—but it certainly was not his mother. Oswald embraced the Marxist philosophy. He dedicated most of the last nine years of his life to studying and espousing its ideals.

Karl Marx, whose socialist philosophy apparently influenced Lee Harvey Oswald to an enormous degree.

Oswald: Marine, Defector, Activist

In 1956, at the age of seventeen, Oswald took his love of Marxism into the Marine Corps. His stint with the marines was undistinguished and lasted almost three years. Fellow marines remember him for reading Marxist literature and being a poor rifle shot. Nelson Delgado, who served with Oswald, called Oswald's shooting ability ''a joke.'' Author Henry Hurt interviewed more than fifty other men who served with Oswald in the marines. Almost to a man, they remember Oswald as having poor rifle skills. More than one of them recalls that Oswald never actually passed his rifle requirements, but was given a passing score anyway so he could continue his marine training.

However, Oswald impressed his superiors in other ways. After he completed basic training he was stationed at a key U.S. air base in Atsugi, Japan. Lieutenant Charles Donovan, one of Oswald's superiors at Atsugi, considered Oswald ''very competent'' and ''brighter than most people.'' Oswald served as a radar operator at Atsugi and worked under a top-secret security clearance. As part of his regular duties, he charted departures and landings of American spy planes. Only a select few marines were entrusted with such an assignment.

As a young Marine, Lee Harvey Oswald was stationed in California where the above picture was taken. In 1958 he worked as a radar operator in Atsugi, Japan (bottom).

In the summer of 1959, another notable aspect of Oswald's marine career emerged: his sudden fluency in the Russian language. In earlier training he had shown only a marginal ability to understand the language. Since then, though, with no formal instruction, he had learned to speak Russian so well that he could pass for a Soviet citizen.

In September 1959, Oswald told the marines that he needed to return to the United States so he could care for his mother. According to Oswald, she was unable to look after herself. The marines granted him an early discharge.

Marguerite Oswald was living in Fort Worth, Texas, at the time. Oswald spent three days there with her, moved on to New Orleans—and promptly hopped a boat bound for France. From France he went to England, from England to Finland, and from Finland Lee Oswald completed his trek by arriving at the border of the Soviet Union. He tried to bargain his way into the country by offering the Soviets U.S. military secrets. To support himself, he worked at a

Marina Oswald stands with her husband Lee on a bridge in Minsk before they chose to return to the United States.

radio factory in the western city of Minsk, 450 miles from the Soviet capital of Moscow.

Oswald quickly lost his enthusiasm for Soviet life. He corresponded with U.S. authorities for a year and a half about arranging his return to the U.S. He finally left the Soviet Union in May 1962. With him when he departed was his new bride, Marina, a nineteen-year-old Soviet girl whom he had married in April, 1961, and the couple's three-month-old daughter. The Oswalds settled in the Dallas area upon their return. In October 1962, just before the Cuban Missile Crisis erupted, Lee started to work at a Dallas graphic arts company that specialized in typesetting jobs for the U.S. Department of Defense. He worked there until April 1963. At that time Oswald left his family in Texas and moved to New Orleans to look for other work.

One of the pamphlets which
Oswald distributed.

After he had found work and a place to live, his wife and daughter joined him in New Orleans.

In New Orleans Oswald adopted another cause: Cuba. On his own, he created an unapproved chapter of the Fair Play for Cuba Committee (FPCC), a pro-Castro organization. He listed his chapter's president as "A.J. Hidell," a name most researchers believe was fictitious. Oswald himself was his chapter's secretary and only active member. He wasted no time in publicizing his FPCC affiliation; he printed and distributed "Hands Off Cuba" flyers shortly after he formed the chapter. In distributing the flyers he angered a group of anti-Castro protesters. A minor scuffle ensued, and Oswald wound up in jail.

While in jail, Oswald made the strange request to speak with someone from the FBI. The FBI investigates possible violations of federal laws. On the surface, a small street corner argument would seem too trivial to interest the FBI. An agent responded to Oswald's request, though, and they spoke in Oswald's jail cell for an hour. No one has ever known what Oswald and the agent spoke about that day.

Oswald quit his job in New Orleans in September 1963. Shortly afterward, his wife and daughter moved to the Dallas suburb of Irving. There they lived with Ruth Paine, a Russian-speaking friend.

Records indicate that Oswald traveled to Mexico City after his wife and daughter returned to Texas.

A photo of Oswald probably taken in September 1963.

He is supposed to have visited the Cuban and Soviet embassies there, asking for entrance visas for both Cuba and the Soviet Union. The normally mild, polite Oswald behaved so rudely at the Cuban embassy that two embassy staff members instantly recognized Oswald's name later in news reports about Kennedy's assassination. After seeing film clips of Oswald, though, both staff members were surprised; they did not recognize the face of the man identified by the news media as Lee Harvey Oswald. Was the man at the Cuban Embassy Oswald—or an impostor? Most assassination researchers, including Anthony Summers, author of *Conspiracy*, strongly suspect that an Oswald imposter visited the embassy. Summers concludes that "today the questions remain. Was somebody impersonating Oswald in Mexico City and, if so, why? There are no easy answers."

Oswald resurfaced in the United States in early October 1963. Since he had no job to return to in New Orleans, he moved to Texas. He left his wife and daughter with Ruth Paine and went to Dallas to look for work. He had barely begun his search when Ruth Paine heard that the Texas School Book Depository had an opening for a warehouse employee. Oswald applied for and got the job. His employment at the depository began October 15, 1963.

Oswald and the Assassination

After his arrest, circumstantial evidence accumulated against Oswald rapidly. Police learned that as early as 12:15, witnesses had seen a gunman on the sixth floor of the depository. Police found a rifle on the sixth floor that was traced to "A.J. Hidell," the same name Oswald had listed as his FPCC chapter's president. The name also was traced to Oswald's Dallas post office box. No fingerprints were found on the rifle; later that weekend, though, the FBI did find a palmprint on the rifle's barrel. The print was Oswald's.

Oswald displays his handcuffed wrists for the press while being led to a cell in the Dallas police station on the night of the assassination.

Evidence like this hurt Oswald. But even more damaging was the fact that he left the depository soon after the assassination. He was the only male employee in the building who did not report for work that afternoon. When he was arrested at 2:00, he was carrying a loaded revolver. Taken together, the "hard" evidence seemed to point to Oswald as a frightened, fleeing assassin.

The Warren Commission examined such evidence and combined it with its own psychological profile of Oswald. The commission concluded that Oswald was Kennedy's lone assassin. Oswald was depicted in the Warren Report as a frustrated, confused political zealot who would have killed a U.S. president just to increase his own tortured self-esteem. This was the official theory of John F. Kennedy's assassination. According to it, the assassination resulted from forces that no one could have predicted or prevented. To the

Warren Commission, it was simply an outcome of Oswald's unstable childhood and his attraction to "un-American" philosophies.

The circumstantial evidence against Oswald was strong; it would have been difficult to deny in any court of law. But ever since the official theory was published in the Warren Report, independent researchers have insisted that Oswald—if he was involved at all—probably had help with the assassination. Josiah Thompson, in *Six Seconds in Dallas*, writes that "it is increasingly unacceptable" that Oswald's rifle "was the *only* weapon fired at the President." According to Thompson's analysis, at least one other gunman fired at Kennedy. Another assassination researcher, Henry Hurt, thinks that "a powerful case can be made that Oswald did *not* kill Kennedy."

A ballistics expert, holding the Mannlicher-Carcano rifle believed to be the assassination weapon, testifies before the House Assassinations Committee.

In 1978, the House Select Committee on Assassinations agreed with such conclusions. The committee thoroughly researched the assassination. It listened to testimony about the assassination for two years. The committee concluded "that President John F. Kennedy was probably assassinated as a result of a conspiracy."

Which conclusion is correct? The official theory? Or one of the conspiracy theories formulated in the decades following the assassination? Did Oswald, acting alone, kill President Kennedy? Or does the circumstantial evidence only hide the more tantalizing evidence of a conspiracy?

The most damaging charge leveled against the Warren Commission was that it did not conduct its inquiry with an open mind. Critics concluded that the commission had assumed from the outset that Oswald was the lone assassin. Such an assumption would have

Senator John Cooper (left) walks with three of the witnesses who gave testimony before the Warren Commission. Next to Cooper is Deputy Sheriff Eugene Boone who conducted the investigation of the School Book Depository. Maurice McDonald, next to Boone, is the Dallas policeman who captured Oswald after the assassination. On the right is policeman Marrion Baker who rushed into the School Book Depository looking for the source of the shots.

greatly affected their investigation. Instead of examining all available evidence before drawing a conclusion, it meant that the commission would look only for evidence that supported its own assumptions about the case.

When critics compared the published Warren Report with the available evidence, they found a multitude of contradictions. The report left little doubt that the Warren Commission thought Oswald had killed Kennedy. The available evidence, however, often sharply contradicted such a conclusion. Even much of the evidence in the commission's own "Hearings and Exhibits" either clouded the certainty of Oswald's guilt or indicated a conspiracy.

The Warren Commission Ignored Evidence

The commission's final report was written as if every shred of evidence proved that Oswald shot Kennedy. The commission ignored even its own evidence if it contradicted the conclusion that Oswald was the lone assassin. To commission critic Sylvia Meagher, the Warren Commission had seemed to *want* to find Oswald, and Oswald alone, guilty of assassinating President Kennedy.

One discrepancy between the Warren Report and the available evidence involved Oswald's marksmanship. The Warren Commission partly based its conclusions on a belief that Oswald was an accomplished marksman. The men who trained with Oswald in the marines, though, remembered him as an unsure, uncoordinated individual who showed little aptitude for firearms. Contrary to such testimony, the Warren Commission found Oswald so skillful with a rifle that he could perform feats of marksmanship that no expert has since been able to duplicate. The marines who served with Oswald laughed at the suggestion. In 1977, Sherman Cooley, a former marine who served with Oswald, voiced little confidence in Oswald's shooting skills:

> If I had to pick one man in the whole United States to shoot me, I'd pick Oswald. I saw that man shoot, and there's no way he could have ever learned to shoot well enough to do what they accused him of.

Comments like Cooley's did not appear in the Warren Report.

Another discrepancy concerned Oswald's precise location at the time of the shooting. He undeniably was in the depository when the shots were fired. But was he on the sixth floor where the rifle and empty shells were recovered? The Warren Commission was satisfied that Oswald was the gunman seen on the sixth floor at 12:15—even though it heard testimony that he very likely was not on that floor immediately before or during the assassination.

An FBI photographer used a camera mounted on the rifle found on the sixth floor of the School Book Depository to re-enact the scene of the assassination. He was attempting to record just what the assassin would have seen.

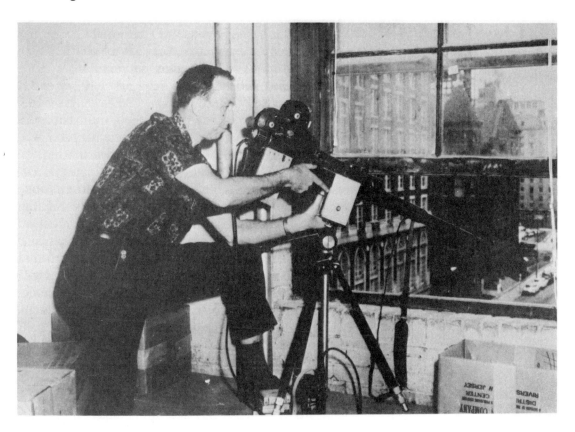

This diagram of the second floor of the School Book Depository building was one of the Warren Commission exhibits. It illustrates the path Oswald was known to have taken on the afternoon of the assassination as well as the assumed route he took. The positions of policeman Marrion Baker and manager Roy Truly are also indicated.

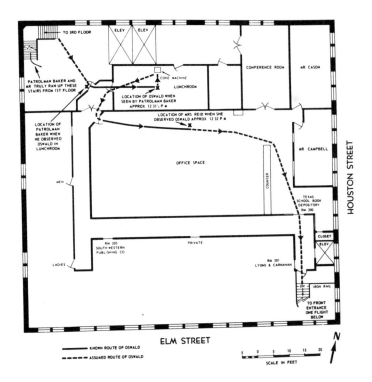

A depository secretary told the commission that she saw Oswald in the building cafeteria between 12:15 and 12:20. (Oswald himself maintained that he was eating lunch at the time of the assassination.) Her testimony directly conflicted with the commission's conclusion that Oswald was the sixth-floor gunman seen by witnesses at 12:15. Critics have pointed out that Oswald could have been in one of the two places at 12:15—either the second-floor cafeteria or the sixth floor—but not both. Instead of taking the secretary's testimony seriously, though, the commission decided that she was "mistaken." Without reservation, the Warren Commission placed Oswald on the depository's sixth floor at the time of the assassination.

Oswald was seen approximately ninety seconds after the shooting by depository manager Roy S. Truly and motorcycle policeman Marrion L. Baker. When he heard the rifle shots, Baker immediately abandoned his motorcycle and raced into the building. Truly volunteered to guide Baker up to the depository's sixth floor.

On the second floor Baker noticed a man walking calmly away from him. According to Baker, the man had just bought a bottle of Coca-Cola. The man was Oswald. He acted so calm in the face of Baker's frantic questioning that neither Baker nor Truly suspected him as the assassin.

This brief confrontation is the source of another discrepancy between the Warren Report and the available evidence. The Warren Commission, having assumed that Oswald was on the sixth floor, tried to prove that he could have walked down to the second floor quickly enough to meet Truly and Baker in the cafeteria. The commission heard testimony that only one person had used the depository stairway immediately after the shooting. That person had seen no one else on the stairway. The only other way Oswald could have reached the cafeteria from the sixth floor was to use one of the building's elevators. All elevators, though, had stopped on floors higher than the second floor after the assassination. If this information is correct, then the only way Oswald could have met Truly and Baker on the second floor was to be there waiting for them.

Oswald's Feverish Escape?

There were other discrepancies. One involved Oswald's absence from the depository the afternoon of the assassination. Oswald said he had gone home to change clothes and go see a movie. He assumed that the depository would be closed that afternoon following the shock of the assassination. He gave no indication that he had fled the building.

In the official theory, however, Oswald's early, unexcused departure was part of a feverish escape. That was the conclusion of the Dallas police and the FBI during the assassination weekend. Later, the

"Ignoring both the glaring and the subtle contradictions, the Warren Commission . . . loaded the dice against (Oswald)."

Author Sylvia Meagher, *Accessories After the Fact*.

"Regardless of what we found, regardless of how the chips might fall, the Chief Justice said, our only concern was for the truth. We took him at his word."

Warren Commission lawyer David W. Belin, *November 22, 1963: You Are the Jury*.

Warren Commission reached the same conclusion, despite hearing testimony that Oswald was calm and at ease before he left the building. Before he left, he spoke briefly and politely with a depository secretary. Less than fifteen minutes later, a taxi driver saw him offer his cab to an elderly lady who needed a ride. In these eyewitness accounts, Oswald is simply a calm, collected young man who left work early on an extraordinary day. Critics have wondered whether this was the same man who was supposed to be fleeing the scene of the assassination.

Did Oswald Kill Tippitt?

Between 1:00 and 1:04, Oswald changed clothes and picked up his Smith and Wesson revolver at his boardinghouse. At about 1:12, a Dallas policeman, J.D. Tippitt, was shot four times at close range by a man with a pistol. The shooting occurred less than one mile from Oswald's boardinghouse. Later that night, witnesses identified Oswald as Tippitt's killer. But they did so only with difficulty and under questionable lineup circumstances. Oswald was the most shabbily dressed man in the lineup, the only one with a swollen bruise over his left eye, and the only one complaining that he was not getting a fair chance. Under such circumstances, he would have stood out prominently from other potential suspects.

At first, ballistics specialists could not positively identify any of the four bullets as having originated from Oswald's gun. One specialist said that Oswald's pistol *could* have fired one of the four bullets recovered from Tippitt's body. Even then, the verdict was inconclusive. The Dallas police, however, charged Oswald with the murder.

After reexamining the evidence, the Warren Commission, too, concluded that Oswald had killed Officer Tippitt. Killing a policeman fit the hypothesis that Oswald, after assassinating Kennedy, was frantically trying to escape. The commission's critics have ques-

Policeman J.D. Tippitt.

tioned such a hypothesis. They think the Tippitt slaying should be investigated without reference to the assassination and without a preconceived belief in Oswald's guilt. When the critics examine the evidence that way, Oswald looks less like a cold-blooded murderer and more like a man caught in a vicious whirlwind of circumstance.

Oswald and Jack Ruby

At midnight that Friday, less than twelve hours after the assassination, the Dallas police held a hectic press conference. Reporters crowded into the small police conference room to hear Oswald himself answer questions about the assassination. Oswald denied that he had killed anyone. He acted as if he did not know that he was accused of assassinating President Kennedy.

The press conference was brief. Shortly after it began, law enforcement officials led Oswald back to

At a midnight press conference, Oswald was quizzed by reporters about his involvement in the assassination.

Dallas County District Attorney Henry Wade (left) answered reporters' questions about the murder charge brought against Oswald.

his jail cell. After Oswald had left the room, Dallas County District Attorney Henry Wade supplied reporters with background information on the prime suspect. At one point, Wade remarked that Oswald was a member of an anti-Castro group. A loud voice from the back of the room corrected him: Oswald actually belonged to a *pro*-Castro organization, the Fair Play for Cuba Committee. The man who volunteered this information, Dallas nightclub owner Jack Ruby, had posed as a reporter to get into the press conference. Less than thirty-six hours later, he would commit murder by firing one well-placed bullet into Oswald's abdomen.

After Oswald's own brutal death, talk about an assassination conspiracy circulated wildly. Ruby said that he had killed Oswald in a fit of passion out of concern for the slain president's wife. He said he did not want Jacqueline Kennedy to have to return to Dallas and suffer the further ordeal of a trial. He insisted that he had not known Oswald before that weekend.

The record, however, strongly suggests that Ruby must have known Oswald—or information about him—before the assassination. Reports have surfaced that the two men—or Ruby and someone who looked like Oswald—had been seen together in early November 1963 in one of Ruby's nightclubs, just weeks before the assassination.

In addition, Ruby's remark at the press conference indicated some previous acquaintance with Oswald. Only twelve hours after the assassination, Ruby already knew that Oswald's affiliations were pro-Castro. At the press conference, neither reporters nor even the district attorney knew the full details of Oswald's background. How did Jack Ruby, of all people, know what group Oswald had worked for earlier that summer in New Orleans? If he did know about Oswald before the assassination, does that mean that both men were part of a larger plot to kill the president? Such questions have persisted since November 1963.

The Official Theory in Retrospect

The possibility of an assassination was unpleasant, especially in America where people are used to electing their leaders in a more civil manner. Good investigators, though, as Robert Blair Kaiser observed in his book on the later assassination of President Kennedy's brother Robert, "look into every possibility, no matter how fantastic." It is generally agreed today that the Warren Commission failed in this respect.

It did not "look into every possibility"; it left the most difficult questions at the heart of the assassination unanswered. Often, it avoided crucial questions altogether or even deliberately clouded them. (For example, it limited its investigation of Oswald's marksmanship to an interview with Nelson Delgado, the man who called Oswald's shooting ability "a joke." Researcher Henry Hurt was able to locate and interview more than fifty of the former marines who served with Oswald. Hurt speculates that the commission deliberately did not look for other marines

"The weight of historical evidence is that (Kennedy's assassination) was a hit by an organized group. I think Oswald was set up and then murdered with the connivance of authorities."

Historian Herbert Aptheker

"The Commission has found no evidence that either Lee Harvey Oswald or Jack Ruby was part of any conspiracy, domestic or foreign, to assassinate President Kennedy."

The Warren Commission Report, September 27, 1964.

because it was afraid that their testimony, like Delgado's, would contradict the official theory. We now know that the commission hurried its investigation, partly because President Johnson wanted all talk of conspiracy put to rest before the 1964 presidential election. In many ways, the official investigation and the official conclusion were seriously flawed.

Yet the so-called official theory still has much evidence in its favor. Some of the circumstantial evidence that accumulated so rapidly in 1963 still points to Oswald's guilt. He might not have fired on President Kennedy that day; but why was his rifle on the sixth floor of his place of employment? He might not have killed Officer Tippitt later that afternoon, either; but why was he carrying a revolver around downtown Dallas only minutes after the second shooting? Oswald aroused more suspicion that day than we normally expect from an innocent man. Despite all the evidence in his favor, we cannot casually dismiss the evidence against him.

Lyndon Baines Johnson took the presidential oath of office aboard the president's plane less than two hours after John Kennedy was assassinated. Did the Warren Commission investigation suffer because Johnson wanted a conclusion before he ran for reelection in 1964?

The evidence in Oswald's favor suggests that the scope of the case is much broader than one lone assassin. The CIA and FBI, for instance, have consistently refused to turn over hundreds of thousands of pages of their assassination files. These agencies say that releasing the material would harm U.S. national security. Critics have wondered how one assassin's personal motives could possibly threaten national security; if Oswald really acted alone, government agencies should have nothing to hide. The classified documents might show that Oswald was in league with others in the assassination. Evidence even suggests that he could have worked for the FBI, the CIA, or both. Neither agency would want its name publicly associated with Oswald. An association between Oswald and either agency could explain why they have withheld their mountainous assassination files.

But even today, Lee Harvey Oswald still is the most visible suspect in the case. Whether he, acting alone, killed John F. Kennedy; whether he killed the president, but had help doing it; or whether he did

Oswald reacts to reporters as he begins a second day of questioning about the assassination.

On Sunday morning, November 23rd, Lee Harvey Oswald was scheduled to be transported from the city to the county jail. As a live television audience watched, Jack Ruby stepped out of the crowd, stuck his gun next to Oswald's ribs, and shot him.

not kill Kennedy but knew who did, most researchers agree that he played some role in the assassination.

To try to clarify that role, some have looked beyond the circumstantial evidence to New Orleans, where Oswald spent the summer of 1963. His associations there raise even more suspicions. While in New Orleans, he developed direct or indirect ties to both organized crime and U.S. intelligence, particularly the CIA. Members of both groups bore a definite hatred for President Kennedy. Oswald, then, is the key to any understanding of the assassination. He will appear and reappear throughout any discussion of possible conspirators in Kennedy's death.

One possible conspirator is Oswald's killer, Jack Ruby. Some of the most intriguing clues in the case involve Ruby and a group with whom he enjoyed a long, friendly acquaintance.

We commonly call that group the Mafia.

Three

For Whom Murder Is a Science—The Mafia Theory

Investigators in murder cases evaluate suspects on the basis of three qualifications. Most people need a motive, at least one compelling reason that will move them enough to commit murder. Even if they have a motive, they still need a means of accomplishing the deed. Finally, suspects must have had an opportunity to kill the victim. Motive, means and opportunity: prime murder suspects exhibit all three.

In an open-minded investigation, the Mafia—the worldwide network of organized crime—quickly emerges as a prime suspect in the assassination of John F. Kennedy. In 1963, this group exhibited all three essential qualifications.

Kennedy Cracks Down on Crime

As a group, the Mafia wanted John Kennedy out of office for one reason: He was bad for their business.

The Kennedy administration attacked organized crime more relentlessly than any presidential administration before or since. In the late 1950s, John Kennedy and his future attorney general, younger brother Robert, had seen firsthand the devastating effects of organized crime. While still a Massachu-

The attorney general and the president hold a private discussion on the White House veranda.

setts senator, John Kennedy served on the McClellan Committee. This committee investigated the relationship between organized crime and American labor unions. Robert Kennedy assisted the committee as its chief counsel. Over the course of the committee's hearings, both Kennedys personally questioned some of America's leading criminals. The evidence they uncovered revealed a dark, seamy underworld marked by gambling, extortion, blackmail, drugs, and murder. Having viewed the evidence so closely, the Kennedys never forgot it.

As attorney general, Robert Kennedy increased the staff at the Justice Department. He also created a special organized crime unit in the department. The president backed his brother's efforts completely, and their increased pressure saw immediate results. Perhaps not coincidently, arrests on racketeering and other charges increased, too. The Justice Department's "wanted" list of known, active criminals grew from forty to twenty-three hundred. In 1960, the year before the Kennedy administration began, only 35 convictions were obtained for offenses connected with organized crime. By 1963, the last year of the Kennedy era, that figure had ballooned to 288.

During the Kennedy administration, the scope of the attorney general's efforts was broad enough to include anyone who aided organized crime in any way. But though the net of Kennedy justice reached far and wide, it directed special attention toward three individuals. Two were bona fide Mafia bosses, the third perhaps the Mafia's most powerful associate. All three had a personal reason to want at least one of the Kennedys dead.

Three Men Moved to Murder

Robert Kennedy's foremost target was Jimmy Hoffa. Hoffa was only indirectly involved with organized crime, but his influence was perhaps even more widespread than that of any Mafia boss.

In the late 1950s, Hoffa used questionable tactics to become head of America's International Brotherhood of Teamsters, the nation's powerful labor union for truckers and warehouse workers. The Teamsters represented a vital component of the American economy. Without truckers to transport merchandise, and without warehouse workers to unpack and inventory merchandise, the American economy would grind to a standstill. Truckers and warehouse workers work in every state in the country, so the person who controls their union exerts an enormous influence nationwide.

As Teamsters president, Hoffa wielded such an influence. And to strengthen it, he combined his Teamsters activities with the criminal activities of the Mafia. In doing so, Hoffa demonstrated that he could support his desires with violent force if necessary.

The extent of Hoffa's and the Teamsters Union's involvement with organized crime is difficult to determine. Hoffa himself freely admitted to friendships with top mob bosses, particularly New Orleans' Carlos Marcello and Miami's Santos Trafficante. A number of incidents also point unmistakably to such

Senator John McClellan, chief counsel Robert Kennedy, and Senator John Kennedy sit together during a session of the McClellan Committee investigation on organized crime.

an association. Hoffa was known, for instance, to have "transferred" $23 million from the Teamsters pension fund to build a plush Mafia retreat in southern California.

During the McClellan Committee hearings, the Kennedy brothers uncovered similar evidence of Hoffa's ties to organized crime. They not only tried to prosecute him for his offenses; they also went out of their way to embarrass and humiliate him. Hoffa's deep, personal hatred for the Kennedys dated from this period. It intensified in 1961 when John Kennedy became president.

Jimmy Hoffa (left) stands next to Anthony Provenzano who was alleged to be a Mafia captain. Here they are welcomed by union members from New Jersey.

In an unguarded moment in 1962, Hoffa once spoke to Edward Partin, a Louisiana Teamster official, about the possibility of killing Robert Kennedy. He even revealed a plan. In it, according to Partin, the attorney general, while riding in an open convertible, would be shot by someone who had no obvious ties to the Teamsters or to Hoffa himself. Hoffa wanted Robert Kennedy to be shot somewhere in the South where both Kennedys already were unpopular. That way, it would be easier to shift the blame for the assassination to someone else.

Tomato Salesman, Mafia Boss

The plot sounded ominously like the events that transpired in Dallas on November 22, 1963. Was it possible that Hoffa, perhaps with help from his Mafia associates, adjusted the target of his original plan and had the president killed instead of the attorney general?

Another of Robert Kennedy's favorite criminal targets was Hoffa's friend, Carlos Marcello. Marcello covered his criminal activities by pretending to be an enterprising New Orleans tomato salesman. In reality, he was the most powerful Mafia chief in New Orleans history. His influence was so broad that his power base stretched west from Louisiana into Texas. No one knows precisely how much money Marcello's illicit businesses were worth. Criminals, after all, do not publicize their income. In 1963, though, the New Orleans Crime Commission estimated that $1.1 *billion* had passed through Marcello's coffers in that year alone. Under Marcello, organized crime earned its reputation as New Orleans's leading "industry."

Marcello's criminal career had only one flaw: he was not a legal resident of the United States. Before the Kennedy administration, no one had dared tempt Marcello's fury by deporting him. Attorney General Kennedy changed that.

In early 1961, only months after he assumed office, Robert Kennedy ordered the immediate de-

Jimmy Hoffa, Teamsters president, concocted a plan to get rid of Robert Kennedy.

A grim-faced Carlos Marcello sits at the witness table while being questioned by a 1961 Senate committee investigating gambling. He refused to answer questions about his occupation and his business deals.

portation of Carlos Marcello. Marcello was flown to Guatemala, a small Central American country Marcello listed as his homeland. He is said to have fumed and ranted against the Kennedy name all the way to Guatemala. Marcello later defied the attorney general and flew back to America. But, by deporting him at all, Robert Kennedy had added personal insult to the injury his efforts already were inflicting on the criminal's flow of income. Marcello is said to have vowed revenge.

How far was he willing to go to gain that revenge? Marcello could not have risen to his powerful position in the Mafia unless he were capable of ordering another man's death. Given his ruthless nature and his personal hatred for Robert Kennedy, ordering the attorney general's assassination in 1963 was well within Marcello's capabilities. He was not so impractical, however, as to let personal feelings interfere with business. Robert Kennedy caused most of Marcello's problems with the federal government. Marcello realized, though, that having the attorney general killed would only leave a larger problem in his place. As the attorney general's brother *and* president of the United States, John Kennedy was that larger problem.

Edward Becker, a former Marcello associate, has testified that Marcello indeed realized the difference between removing the president from office and removing the attorney general. Becker recalled Marcello's graphic description of the Mafia's ''Kennedy problem''—and his chilling prescription for its solution.

At right is Marcello who is waiting in Guatemala with a government official in charge of deporting him from the country. Marcello had already been deported from the U.S. to Guatemala.

Attorney General Robert Kennedy.

According to Becker, he, Marcello, and two other men were socializing one day in 1962 at a Marcello hideaway when conversation turned to the Kennedys. Marcello plainly expressed his hatred for Robert Kennedy. But he also gave Becker the distinct impression that he saw his "Kennedy problem" from a broader perspective. Marcello remarked that "the dog will keep biting you if you only cut off its tail." To solve the entire problem, he observed, the dog's *head* would have to be removed. Then "the entire dog would die." Marcello realized that having Robert Kennedy killed —"cutting off the tail"—would only invite the wrath of the highest elected official in the country, the president. Killing the president, however, would neutralize Robert Kennedy's effectiveness as attorney general. Without full presidential support, his broad legal authority would shrivel to more modest dimensions.

The Open Convertible—A Mafia Plot?

Marcello's shrewd awareness of the federal power structure invites comparison of his comments with those of his good friend, Jimmy Hoffa. Hoffa apparently originally conceived the assassination plan involving the open convertible for Robert Kennedy. Yet that is exactly how John Kennedy was assassinated. Is it possible that Marcello and Hoffa conspired to have President Kennedy killed? Could Marcello have convinced Hoffa that removing the president would benefit them more than removing the attorney general? After the assassination, Hoffa, too, showed an awareness of the attorney general's newly restricted authority. Hoffa was overheard saying that "Bobby Kennedy's just another lawyer now." Did he arrive at such a realization on his own, or did Marcello help him see the broader perspective?

Another Mafia leader who hated both Kennedys was Santos Trafficante. Trafficante was head of Miami's lucrative organized crime market. Before

Castro rose to power in 1959, Trafficante also conducted extensive criminal operations in Cuba. His Cuban activities included gunrunning. His Cuban fortunes faded, though, after Castro's revolution. Castro wanted to close the market for organized crime in his country. He started by trying to drive all organized crime figures out of Cuba. As a result, Trafficante landed in a Cuban jail in the summer of 1959. Eventually he was expelled from the country.

The United States to which he returned was only slightly more tolerant of organized crime than Cuba had become—and U.S. tolerance, too, was due to end soon. Congressional hearings like those of the McClellan Committee had raised public awareness of organized crime's pervasive influence in America. And, in 1960, anti-crime John Kennedy was elected president. First Cuba, then the United States: Such a trend hampered the Mafia's and Trafficante's productivity.

But early in the Kennedy administration, a government agency and the Mafia found a common objective. The U.S. government preferred that someone besides Castro serve as Cuba's premier. The Mafia, with an eye toward reopening a productive market, held the same preference. At the time, the CIA was launching a variety of assassination plots against Castro. When they realized that they needed help, one of their first contacts was Santos Trafficante.

Even Trafficante-CIA plots against Castro failed. Trafficante's involvement in these plots, though, establishes a precedent for students of John Kennedy's assassination. Trafficante's desire to reopen the Cuban crime market led him to participate in plots to kill Fidel Castro. As a Mafia boss, he already hated the Kennedys for their strict stand against organized crime. He also bore a more personal hatred toward them for Robert Kennedy's consistent pressure against two of his friends, Hoffa and Marcello. Combined with his anti-Kennedy sentiment, Trafficante's desire to unclog the American market might have compelled him to plot President Kennedy's assassination, too.

There is evidence that he entertained such thoughts. In 1962, Trafficante volunteered to help Jose Aleman, a Cuban exile who lived in Miami, obtain a $1 million loan. The loan would be illegally procured from Teamsters Union funds. Trafficante informed Aleman that the loan already "had been cleared by Jimmy Hoffa."

Their conversation turned to the Kennedys' recent efforts at stopping organized crime. According to Aleman, Trafficante voiced a grim prediction about the fate of John Kennedy:

> Mark my words, this man Kennedy is in trouble, and he will get what is coming to him. . . .Kennedy's not going to make it to the [1964] election. He is going to be hit.

According to Aleman, Trafficante spoke of Ken-

nedy's impending death as if it were a foregone conclusion—as if it were already planned and waited only its execution.

Many Means and One Golden Opportunity

The Mafia then, had ample motive to assassinate John Kennedy. But did they possess the means and expertise of doing so, and did they have an opportunity?

Volume after volume of well-documented evidence establishes that murder is a routine Mafia solution for people who "cause problems." Their more common weapons include firearms, knives, and clubs. According to author Anthony Summers, a more extensive roster would include ice picks, blow torches,

Cuban exile Jose Aleman, who once fought with Castro's guerrillas, told investigators for the House Assassinations Committee. what he knew about organized crime and Kennedy's assassination.

and meat hooks. It also would include concrete caskets in which live victims are sealed and dropped to the bottoms of lakes or oceans. This bizarre catalogue of weapons is not fictitious. Chicago Mafia boss Sam Giancana and his associates used all of these weapons. There is no reason to think that a similar list could not be compiled for other members of organized crime.

Top-level leaders like Marcello and Trafficante, or even their close associate, Hoffa, would not be apt

Sam Giancana is handcuffed to a chair while awaiting questioning about the murder of a Chicago banker.

to use such weapons themselves. Traditionally, they would "put out a contract" and hire someone else to commit murder for them. One way or another, such men could have had John Kennedy killed by any of a number of different means.

The final qualification for prime murder suspects is opportunity. The White House announced its general Texas itinerary, including the final stop in Dallas, in early November 1963. Against Secret Service advice, Dallas newspapers printed Kennedy's motorcade route twice during the week before the assassination. Few could have known it at the time, but these announcements gave a potential assassin a chance to prepare in detail for Kennedy's scheduled stop in Dallas.

Kennedy's limousine also worked against the president. Kennedy rode that day without any protective covering over the car. He thought the American voters should be able to see their leader face to face. Without any overhead protection, though, the president of the United States sat completely at the mercy of the throngs of people who lined the Dallas streets.

Any gunman in Dealey Plaza that day—especially a professional Mafia assassin—enjoyed a clear, unobstructed opportunity to kill John Kennedy.

Jack Ruby: Mafia Sidekick

Crime was Jack Ruby's most consistent line of work. As a youngster in Chicago he ran occasional errands for the notorious gangster Al Capone. In the late 1930s he worked as a union organizer for Paul Dorfman. Robert Kennedy called Dorfman "a major operator in the Chicago underworld." In the mid-1940s Ruby moved to Dallas to open a nightclub. At about the same time, the Chicago Mafia decided to expand into fresh territory. Of all the cities they could have chosen to infiltrate, they chose Dallas. Police later learned that they planned to run their illegal operations through Jack Ruby's nightclub. According to a

"Muted in the (Warren) Report, but revealed in the Exhibits, are Ruby's ties with the underworld, gamblers and hoods, (and) narcotics traffic."

Author Sylvia Meagher, *Accessories After the Fact*.

"The Commission believes that the evidence does not establish a significant link between Ruby and organized crime."

The Warren Commission Report, September 27, 1964.

Jack Ruby's nightclub, The Carousel Club, was closed in honor of John Kennedy's memory.

Dallas acquaintance of Ruby, the Mafia *sent* Ruby to Dallas for the express purpose of helping them expand. He continued to run nightclubs until November 24, 1963, but his main career was the crime that supported his more legitimate businesses.

Ruby's criminal activities intensified throughout the 1950s and early 1960s. In 1957, when he started running guns to Cuba, his contacts included representatives of Santos Trafficante. Ruby might even have dealt personally with the Miami Mafia chief. (When

Trafficante was imprisoned in Cuba in 1959, according to a fellow prisoner, "a man named Ruby" visited him.)

Three weeks before the assassination Jack Ruby placed a call to New Orleans for a man named Nofio Pecora. Pecora was one of Carlos Marcello's top aides. A week later Ruby received a call from Barney Baker. Robert Kennedy called Baker Jimmy Hoffa's "roving ambassador of violence." The next day, Ruby called Baker—after he called another key Hoffa associate in Miami.

Did the calls involve last minute details of the assassination? Or was Jack Ruby simply renewing old friendships in the autumn of 1963? Whatever his reasons for calling, his long-distance telephone usage escalated dramatically that fall. An alarming number of those calls were to people who were deeply involved in organized crime.

Interview from the Dallas Jail

Ruby's finances might have made him particularly vulnerable to Mafia influence in 1963. He suffered that year from a chronic shortage of money. He was $44,000 behind in federal income tax payments. He had been missing rent payments on his nightclub buildings before the assassination. But after living on minimal funds all year, Ruby appeared at his Dallas bank on the afternoon of November 22 with a pocketful of large-denomination bills. Sunday, November 24, after he killed Oswald, police found $3,000 on his person and in his car. Later, in a session with a psychiatrist, he said that he had been "framed into killing Oswald." If he was indeed "framed," is it possible that money was involved? Could his Mafia associates have persuaded him to kill Oswald by offering him money? If that is possible, could the Mafia also have threatened to kill Ruby himself if he did not carry out his task?

Ruby's bizarre testimony before the Warren Commission in June 1964 has aroused even more suspicion about his role in the events surrounding Kennedy's assassination. Commission members Earl Warren and Gerald Ford interviewed Ruby in his Dallas jail cell. Again and again, Ruby expressed mortal fear to the commissioners; he expected to die in the Dallas jail soon after they heard his testimony. The fact that he was speaking to them at all, he said, was enough to jeopardize not only his own life, but those of his relatives as well. Eight times Ruby interrupted his testimony to beg the commission to realize the danger he was in if he remained in Dallas:

> Gentlemen, my life is in danger here.
> I want to tell the truth, and I can't tell it here. I can't tell it here.
> Gentlemen, unless you get me to Washington, you can't get a fair shake out of me.

If Ruby did kill Oswald on Mafia orders, was it possible that he expected the mob to "silence" him, too, once he had fulfilled his role in the conspiracy? Ruby's background had taught him that the Mafia can reach its victims anywhere. He knew that if the Mafia wanted someone dead, not even a guarded jail cell could provide sanctuary. Someone inspired immense terror in Jack Ruby after he killed Oswald; if not the Mafia, who? That is another question that no one has answered with certainty in all the years since the assassination.

Someone to Finish the Job?

Jack Ruby associated with men who voiced a desire to kill President Kennedy. He spoke with close aides of Carlos Marcello and Jimmy Hoffa. He ran guns to Cuba through representatives of Santos Traficante. In addition to having a motive to kill Kennedy, these men were experienced in a variety of effective ways of committing murder. They had ample opportunity to arrange the president's death that Friday in Dallas. Did any—or all three—of them help

plot the assassination? If so, could they have feared that Lee Harvey Oswald would reveal too much information to the authorities after his arrest? If they did want to silence Oswald, is it possible that they enlisted an old Dallas contact, someone they knew they could count on to "finish the job"?

An obviously distressed Jack Ruby is led to a sanity hearing after his conviction for shooting Oswald. Was he afraid that his Mafia connections would silence him?

Lee Harvey Oswald and the Mafia

What, if anything, did Lee Harvey Oswald know about a plot to kill John F. Kennedy? The Warren Commission said he could not possibly have known of a plot because there was no plot. It concluded that Oswald, and Oswald alone, was responsible for Kennedy's death. For the Mafia theorists, however, there was a plot, and for the Mafia theory to work at all Oswald must have known some of the plot's components. The lone-assassin theorists believe Ruby's explanation; they dismiss Oswald's death as an act of immediate, unplanned passion. Mafia theorists, on the other hand, see it as the final strand in an intricately spun conspiracy.

Even today, it is still almost impossible to tell what Oswald could have known about a Mafia conspiracy. A much easier question to answer is *how* and *through whom* he might have learned such information. One period of Oswald's short life is particularly fruitful in this line of inquiry. From April to October 1963, Oswald lived in his birthplace, New Orleans. From May to September of that year he worked at the William B. Reily Company as an oiler of coffee-making machinery. As a Reily employee, Oswald

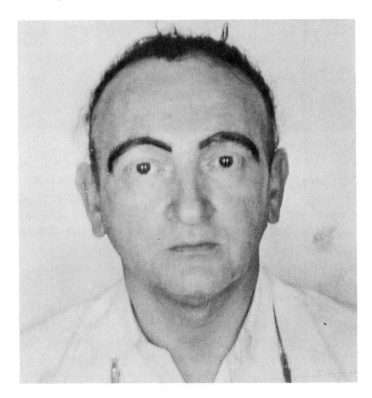

New Orleans "mug shots" of David Ferrie. Did he work for the CIA as well as for the Mafia? What part did he play in the mystery of the Kennedy assassination?

worked within walking distance of more clandestine activities. Evidence suggests that he participated in them.

The William B. Reily Company sat within a city block of a building out of which a man named David W. Ferrie worked. Ferrie, almost twice Oswald's age, was eccentric in both actions and appearance. He suffered from a disease which caused a complete lack of body hair; to compensate, he resorted to wigs and fake eyebrows. He read widely, was familiar with a number of religions and psychologies, and held an airplane pilot's license. He strongly favored conservative politics and vehemently opposed John Kennedy's presidency. He also opposed Cuba's Fidel Castro and sympathized with New Orleans's community of anti-Castro Cuban exiles. There is evidence that Ferrie helped the CIA train the anti-Castro

"Oswald's accessibility to both organized crime and the anti-Castro movement was represented in his association with assassination suspect David Ferrie."

Author David E. Scheim, *Contract on America.*

"Numerous reports surfaced of witnesses who could link Oswald with David Ferrie. . . . Unfortunately many of these reports come from sources who must be considered unreliable, and who might have had reasons of their own for exaggerating this link."

Author Paul L. Hoch, The Rockefeller Commission, March 24, 1975.

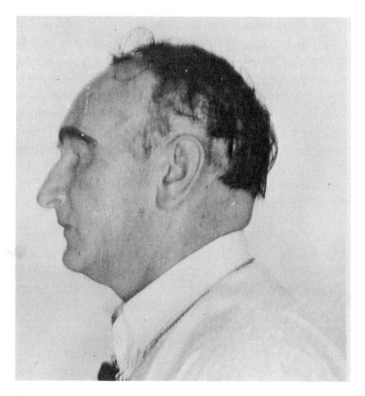

guerrillas for the 1961 Bay of Pigs invasion. It is also possible that he flew for the guerrillas during the invasion. He, too, felt betrayed by John Kennedy.

This strange, bitter man also acted as a special aide to one of New Orleans's most powerful citizens, Carlos Marcello. Ferrie was rumored to have piloted Marcello's return from Guatemala in 1961.

In November 1963, Ferrie served as an investigator for one of Marcello's attorneys to help defend the mobster in a criminal case. Around noon on November 22, 1963, Ferrie sat with Marcello in a New Orleans courtroom to hear a jury set Marcello free. Three days later, after hearing that he was a suspect in the assassination, he turned himself in for questioning. The New Orleans district attorney, the FBI, and the Secret Service all questioned Ferrie. He was released shortly thereafter.

Oswald's Connection to Ferrie

Researchers are certain of a connection between Ferrie and Oswald during Oswald's summer stay in New Orleans in 1963. Before Oswald distributed his pro-Castro flyers in August, he stamped some of them with an address for his Fair Play for Cuba Committee chapter's headquarters. The address he used was 544 Camp Street—the same address of the building out of which David Ferrie worked.

Also in the building was a retired FBI agent, Guy Banister, whose political views were identical to Ferrie's. Both men hated John Kennedy passionately. Banister, too, had helped U.S. intelligence agents organize the anti-Castro exiles; in fact, he was still helping them in the summer of 1963.

Delphine Roberts, Banisters' secretary, remembers that Oswald was in the building often. She also says that he commonly spoke with Ferrie and Banister. Why was Lee Harvey Oswald, a simple coffee-factory worker and supporter of Castro, involved with people who sought to overthrow the Cuban leader? If

HANDS OFF CUBA!

Join the Fair Play for Cuba Committee

NEW ORLEANS CHARTER MEMBER BRANCH

Free Literature, Lectures

LOCATION:

L. H. OSWALD
4907 MAGAZINE ST
NEW ORLEANS, LA.

EVERYONE WELCOME!

Commission Exhibit 2966-A

This shot of Lee Harvey Oswald distributing the "Hands Off Cuba" pamphlet in New Orleans was taken from a 16mm movie film.

Oswald's pro-Castro sympathies were sincere, Ferrie and Banister should have been his enemies. Yet he regularly spoke at length with them. He worked alongside them. He perhaps even worked *for* them. It is possible that Oswald faked his pro-Castro activities. If he did, those activities could have been parts of espionage projects with U.S. intelligence agencies. In the Mafia theory, though, Oswald's association with Ferrie can be explained more easily.

Author David Scheim believes that Ferrie's client, Carlos Marcello, masterminded John Kennedy's assassination. According to Scheim, both Oswald and Ferrie "left a trail that led . . . to New Orleans Mafia boss Carlos Marcello."

In 1962, when Marcello spoke of "cutting off the dog's head," he mentioned how easy it would be to cover up Mafia involvement, even in a presidential assassination. According to Edward Becker, Marcello said that all one had to do was "set up a nut to take the blame." Through David Ferrie, Marcello could have known about Oswald, a man who has gone down in history as the "lone nut" who killed John F. Kennedy.

Weighing the Mafia Theory

Many groups hated John Kennedy in 1963. None of them displayed the combination of economic and personal motives found in the Mafia. John Kennedy was the ultimate source of power for the attorney general who pursued organized crime figures. In particular, he was the source of power for the attorney general who made Jimmy Hoffa and Carlos Marcello two of his pet criminal projects. Eventually, John Kennedy, as America's highest elected official, became the target of vicious intentions for the people his brother pursued. That much is on the historical record.

An indirect relationship between Lee Harvey Oswald and the Mafia is on the record, too. The fact that he associated with David Ferrie in New Orleans in the summer of 1963 is beyond dispute. It is possible to establish a point of contact, but it is difficult to say what Oswald might have known that would have forced the Mafia to murder him. If there was a plot, could Oswald have known its details? Could he have known who was involved? Did he realize, after his arrest,

This overhead view of President Kennedy's car in the Dallas motorcade illustrates how unprotected he was. Could Jimmy Hoffa and Mafia boss Carlos Marcello have changed plans and decided to murder John instead of Robert Kennedy?

that he had been "set up" (as his statements that he was "just a patsy" seem to indicate)? To this day, no one knows. Even though it is seriously flawed and incomplete, the only "hard" evidence still points to Oswald as a lone assassin. Like every other theory about John F. Kennedy's death, the Mafia theory only tantalizes researchers where they would prefer certainty.

But, as supporters of the Mafia theory point out, researchers should expect a degree of uncertainty where organized crime is involved. In a trademark Mafia "hit," evidence is either so scarce or so conflicting that the case persistently defies successful investigation. In Kennedy's assassination, there is a surplus of available evidence. The trouble is that it leads to a number of different conclusions; in many ways, each conclusion is as plausible as the next.

David Scheim sees the dark hand of the Mafia behind this web of confusion. Other researchers—like Anthony Summers, Henry Hurt, and David S. Lifton—think such conflict could just as easily point to other groups for whom stealth, assassination, and manipulation of evidence are possible. These other groups—the CIA, the FBI, and the Secret Service—are all agencies of the U.S. government. All have played questionable roles in the assassination investigation. Their silence on what was officially an "open-and-shut" case has caused widespread suspicion that they, too, could have participated in the events of November 22, 1963.

Four

When the President's Men Rebelled—The U.S. Intelligence Theories

Coup d'etat is a French term that literally means "stroke of state." It dates from what is usually considered a more barbaric time when disputes were settled by strokes of a sword. Metaphorically, a *coup d'etat* is a violent "swordstroke" that changes a state's, or nation's, government. The term refers to one segment of an existing government rising up to overthrow the ruling party.

Some researchers explain Kennedy's assassination in similar terms. Like Mafia theorists, advocates of a state conspiracy theory do not see Kennedy's death as the work of one crazed, desperate assassin. They think that Lee Harvey Oswald probably played some role in the assassination. But they also contend that he, by himself, could not have arranged the wildly conflicting evidence that still baffles investigators today. Successful *coups d'etat* result from careful design and a pooling of many people's talents and resources.

Most researchers do not think that any government agency officially sanctioned Kennedy's assassination. What scant evidence does exist suggests only that a "renegade element" in the U.S. intelligence community *might* have been involved with

President Kennedy signs an official proclamation putting into effect a blockade on Cuba.

the assassination. If entire government agencies like the CIA, the FBI, and the Secret Service had been involved, intelligence theorists say, too many people would have known about the plot to carry it out undetected.

That leaves the possibility of individuals within these agencies deciding on their own to kill John Kennedy. Supporting evidence for such a hypothesis does not conclusively prove that U.S. intelligence agents were involved in the assassination. But, as state conspiracy theorists point out, it does not conclusively prove that they were not involved, either.

The CIA: Spies or Executioners?

The Bay of Pigs fiasco in April 1961 caused bitterness and distrust on all sides. The anti-Castro exiles and their CIA sponsors resented Kennedy's refusal to order American military participation in the invasion. For his part, the president resented the CIA for intentionally misleading him about the strength of Castro's support in Cuba.

The CIA's pre-invasion reports assured Kennedy that the exiles could topple Castro's young government handily once they established a beachhead at the Bay of Pigs. As Kennedy found out later, the CIA reports were grossly inaccurate; Castro's support and military resistance were formidable. Top CIA personnel at the time were in favor of U.S. military involvement in Cuba. They expected the president to send in American troops when he realized how badly Castro's forces outnumbered the exiles. Kennedy trusted their reports and expected the exiles to succeed in overthrowing Castro. He did not budge from his pre-invasion pledge to keep American troops out of the invasion. When the invasion crumbled, Kennedy realized how greatly he had been misled. He vowed to "splinter the CIA into a thousand pieces and scatter it to the winds."

Such an atmosphere of mutual distrust and resent-

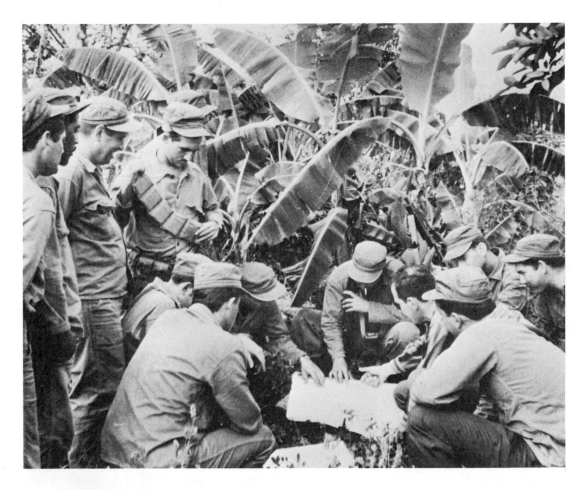

ment could have encouraged some CIA personnel to plot Kennedy's death. If this is a likely motive, then the CIA operatives most likely to participate were the ones involved in the Bay of Pigs invasion. And for assistance, they could have turned to a man who helped them in the invasion, a man easy to remember for his lack of hair and rabidly conservative politics, David Ferrie.

Ferrie often spoke about the benefits of killing John Kennedy. Once, during a speech, he was asked to leave the podium because of the strength of his attacks on Kennedy. The degree of his anti-Kennedy

Anti-Castro forces plan their strategy before the invasion of Cuba. The CIA assured the president that these forces could depose Castro easily, but when they didn't, a permanent rift developed between Kennedy and the CIA.

sentiments is especially alarming for one so closely allied with U.S. intelligence through the CIA. In 1960 and 1961, Ferrie reportedly helped the CIA train anti-Castro Cuban exiles for the Bay of Pigs invasion. But Ferrie's involvement with the Bay of Pigs project might not have stopped with the training of guerillas. He reportedly flew in the invasion but could not land because the ground was swarming with pro-Castro forces.

There is evidence that Ferrie worked for the CIA at other times, too. Victor Marchetti, former executive assistant to the deputy director of the CIA, is "absolutely convinced that Ferrie was a CIA contract officer and involved in some rather nefarious activities." In addition to his Mafia clients, then, David Ferrie probably worked for the CIA, too.

What exactly was the extent of Ferrie's CIA affiliations? In the years following the assassination, that

Air force officers who were part of the Cuban surveillance team brief the president before the Bay of Pigs invasion.

question has become almost impossible to answer. No mention of Ferrie in declassified CIA files indicates that he was an agent. But, as a confidential source once said, "in intelligence work, that is not unusual." Given his political beliefs and his CIA connections, many researchers wonder if the CIA's undisclosed files show that Ferrie was an agent who did indeed play a role in the assassination.

Was Oswald a CIA Scapegoat?

Lee Harvey Oswald figures heavily in the CIA conspiracy theory, too. As in the Mafia theory, he is a convenient scapegoat, a pawn manipulated by higher powers so they would not shoulder the blame for the assassination. Researchers like Anthony Summers and Henry Hurt have examined the many unexplained gaps of Oswald's background in great detail. They conclude that someone, probably the CIA, could have sponsored his activities as early as his stint in the Marine Corps.

The murky details of Oswald's life have caused much speculation about the "full story" on him. He was relatively uneducated. He was poor. Such a background usually means that a person will not be interested in world travel. Or, if they are, their relative poverty will keep them from traveling.

Yet neither of these points applied to Oswald. He traveled through many countries with ease and apparently without a second thought about the money involved. Does this mean that he received encouragement and financial help in his travels? Were Oswald's travels concealed spy missions for the CIA? The evidence is inconclusive. But, as Henry Hurt has pointed out, if Oswald was involved in intelligence activities we could not reasonably expect to find evidence of his participation. Such evidence would have been destroyed so that Oswald could maintain his "cover." Proving or disproving a CIA-Oswald rela-

David Ferrie was found dead in his apartment shortly before he was scheduled to be arrested in an assassination conspiracy investigation headed by New Orleans District Attorney Jim Garrison.

tionship, then, with complete certainty either way, is all but impossible. For instance, Oswald's 1959 defection to the Soviet Union could have been part of a CIA program designed to plant U.S. spies in the middle of day-to-day life in the Soviet Union. But the fact that Oswald did defect to the Soviet Union so easily does not "prove" that anyone sponsored his defection. In this instance, an Oswald-CIA connection is only speculation. Other evidence, though, strengthens the hypothesis that Oswald was a low-level CIA operative before the assassination.

Links Between Oswald and the CIA

After the assassination, the CIA denied having any prior knowledge of Oswald. Subsequent investigation has shown that those denials were false. The CIA maintained a "201" file on Oswald perhaps as early as 1960. The agency has explained that 201 files were kept on anyone who might be able to provide significant information that would affect U.S. national security. According to the CIA, Oswald, as a defector, was a routine subject for a 201. Two things, though, are disturbing about Oswald's 201. First, the government initially denied its existence. Beyond that, although the original date on the file is 1960, the file's 1960 entries obviously refer to events that did not happen until 1962—events no one could have foreseen in 1960. Did the CIA destroy its original Oswald file and hastily reconstruct another? If so, why?

Another area that suggests a link between Oswald and the CIA is Oswald's September 1963 trip to Mexico City. Travelers to Mexico needed "tourist cards" to enter the country. On September 17, 1963, Oswald applied for and received his tourist card at the Mexican consulate in New Orleans. At the Warren Commission's request, the FBI investigated Oswald's tourist card application in the consulate's files. The Bureau noticed something strange about the files: One name was missing. Perhaps it was only coincidence, but the

Former CIA agent Victor Marchetti firmly believes that David Ferrie did "contract" work for the CIA.

Former CIA Director Richard Helms testified before the House Assassinations Committee. How much did he and other CIA officials know about Oswald? Did the CIA sponsor Oswald's defection to the Soviet Union?

missing name belonged to the person who applied for the tourist card just before Oswald's.

For years, government officials said that it *was* only a coincidence. Then, in 1975, the whole tourist card episode began to look like more than just coincidence. That year, the missing name was mistakenly released during declassification of other government documents; the government had had possession of the missing name all along. Further research into the name suggests that its suppression for so long might not have been coincidence at all.

The name that turned up was William G. Gaudet —a long-time CIA informant on Latin American affairs. Gaudet traveled to Mexico City at the same time

This is the man the CIA identified as Lee Harvey Oswald. Pictures of this man were supposed to have been taken outside the Cuban Embassy in September 1963. Compare him to the pictures of Oswald on the opposite page. Why did the CIA claim this was Oswald?

Oswald did in 1963. His appearance in Oswald's background has only fueled speculation that Oswald worked in some capacity for the CIA. Did Oswald and Gaudet travel to Mexico City for the same purpose? Was the trip to Mexico City part of a CIA assignment?

Despite its early claims to the contrary, the CIA did know about the trip. Gaudet might or might not have been involved in an assignment with Oswald. What is certain is that the CIA took photographs of a man they identified as Oswald outside the Cuban embassy in Mexico City. When confronted with the fact that the man was not Oswald, the agency denied further comment. They never have identified the swarthy man they originally called Lee "Henry" Oswald. Was the CIA genuinely mistaken? Were they really unaware that the man they photographed was not Oswald? Is it possible that they took the photo intentionally, to help cover Oswald's movements in Mexico City? If Oswald did work for the CIA, the agency would have needed to protect his identity. Intentionally misnaming the man in the photo—by calling him

Oswald—could have been an attempt to confuse foreign intelligence agencies.

The important question when studying the assassination is not whether the CIA knew Oswald before November 22, 1963. Oswald's 201 file proves that they did. The important question is how certain members of the CIA could have used Oswald in a plot to kill Kennedy. It is possible that the CIA misled Oswald to believe that he was involved in a plot to kill Fidel Castro. That could be why he traveled to Mexico City and demanded a Cuban entrance visa. According to this scenario, Oswald faked his pro-Castro activities as part of a far-reaching CIA plot of which he was only partially aware. Once he had publicly established pro-Castro sympathies, the CIA could then arrange Kennedy's death; they could paint Oswald, a supporter of one of Kennedy's bitterest rivals, as the assassin. It would look like Oswald had killed Kennedy out of sympathy for the Cuban premier —or so the theory goes.

COMMISSION EXHIBIT 2891

COMMISSION EXHIBIT 2892

These photos were part of the Warren Commission exhibit files. They were taken in the Soviet Union during Oswald's stay from 1959 to 1962.

Responsible investigators say we may never know if the CIA plotted the assassination. The evidence is too incomplete, and it does not promise to improve. What files the agency has declassified and released to the public contain nagging discrepancies with the official explanation of Kennedy's death. Perhaps even more disturbing is the CIA's consistent refusal to release all of its assassination documents. (In 1985, Henry Hurt estimated that all unreleased government files—including the CIA's—contain more than 500,000 pages of central information on the case.) At the very least, the agency's refusal casts strong suspicion on itself. If the official theory is true, then the CIA should have nothing to hide. It could erase all doubt about its role in the assassination by revealing its pertinent evidence. Instead the CIA has shown only that it prefers secrecy in the case, even if that means enduring the risk of public suspicion.

The FBI: Investigation or Cover-up?

Some evidence strongly suggests direct CIA involvement in the assassination; yet, on the whole, it is weak enough that it can only be called inconclusive. When looking at other intelligence-related agencies, however, the evidence becomes weaker still. There is virtually no "hard" evidence, for instance, that the FBI helped (or wanted to help) kill John Kennedy. The FBI's role in the assassination seems limited to its function of investigation. Most researchers do not suspect the FBI as a source of Kennedy's assassin. What they do suggest is that it has deliberately kept the truth of the case hidden from public view.

The FBI attracted suspicion early in the investigation. One of its first statements about the assassination was that it knew nothing of Oswald before November 22, 1963. Subsequent research has proven that statement to be false. As early as June 26, 1962, thirteen days after Oswald's return from the Soviet Union, the FBI conducted the first of several inter-

views with him. Before the summer was over they contacted him again. The agency was concerned that the Soviets might have recruited Oswald as a spy during his defection. According to the FBI, such contact with returned defectors is routine.

The FBI paid other, less routine visits to Oswald, though. Taken individually, they might excite little suspicion. But when placed in the context of all FBI contact with Oswald—and in the context of Oswald's cloudy biography—the FBI's continued contact with him seems more than routine. In addition to his other activities, it is also possible that Lee Harvey Oswald worked for the FBI as an informant.

Two incidents in particular support this conclusion. Both occurred during Oswald's busy stay in New Orleans between April and September 1963. In the

FBI Director William Webster was asked to testify before the House Assassinations Committee. How much did Webster and the FBI know about Oswald, how much did they deliberately keep secret?

first incident, a New Orleans garage manager, Adrian Alba, saw Oswald accepting a package from a man Alba recognized as an FBI agent. Alba's garage had a contract with the government to work on unmarked cars for the FBI and Secret Service. Alba had rented a car to an FBI agent the day before he saw Oswald accepting the package. It was easy for him to recognize both the car and the driver when the car stopped at a curb the next day beside Oswald. He recognized Oswald, too, because Oswald regularly stopped by Alba's garage to chat. For these reasons, Alba's story seems reliable. What would Oswald have been receiving from an FBI agent?

The second incident is even more certain because it is part of the public record. On August 9, 1963, Oswald was arrested for fighting with anti-Castro partisans who opposed his distribution of pro-Castro leaflets. The next day, while still in jail, he requested to speak to someone from the FBI. Agent John L.

Marina Oswald, Lee Harvey's wife, appeared before the Warren Commission to tell them what she knew.

Quigley responded to the request. He spoke to Oswald in his jail cell for more than an hour. Quigley's report noted that Oswald voiced strong support for Castro; at one point he even showed the agent his FPCC membership card. Could this interview have been a CIA ploy that allowed Oswald to more firmly establish his pro-Castro credentials? Or was the jail-cell interview part of Oswald's regular contact with the FBI? Perhaps he had learned new information about New Orleans's anti-Castro community during the scuffle. If Oswald was an FBI informant, this was the kind of information the Bureau would have expected Oswald to pass along to them. Did he arrange the interview so he could report his findings to Agent Quigley?

The FBI tried to investigate Oswald at least one other time before the assassination. On November 1, 1963, Agent James P. Hosty Jr., went to Ruth Paine's Irving home to interview Oswald's wife, Marina. The FBI was trying to confirm Marina's status in the United States. Was she simply the innocent wife of a book warehouse worker, or was she performing some intelligence function for her home country, the Soviet Union? The FBI man questioned Marina while Ruth Paine interpreted. (Marina Oswald spoke little English at the time). Hosty directed most of his inquiries that day toward Marina's activities. He also tried, indirectly, to elicit information from Marina about her husband.

FBI Denies Knowing Oswald

The record clearly shows that the FBI spoke to Oswald before the assassination on numerous occasions. Why, then, just after the assassination, did the Bureau deny any previous knowledge of the prime suspect? Why, less than two hours after Ruby killed Oswald, did FBI director J. Edgar Hoover express a strange eagerness to show that Oswald, and Oswald alone, was guilty of killing the president? When

J. Edgar Hoover was very eager to prove Oswald the lone assassin. Why?

The Warren Commission presents its findings to President Lyndon B. Johnson.

Hoover heard the news of Oswald's death, he telephoned President Johnson with an urgent message:

> The thing I am most concerned about . . . is having something issued so we can convince the public that Oswald is the real assassin.

Hoover made this comment less than forty-eight hours after the assassination investigation began. Was he hasty in wanting to end the investigation so soon? Many people think so. There are three important questions about Hoover's "official" conclusion (the same conclusion the Warren Commission arrived at ten months later in its 1964 report). Was this some form of cover-up? And, if so, what were federal officials hiding—and why did they want to hide it?

Hoover could not possibly have known every relevant fact about the assassination on November 24. He therefore could not have known with certainty that Oswald, and Oswald alone, was "the real assassin." It is possible that Hoover and other top federal officials—perhaps even President Johnson—wanted to calm the American public's fears so soon after the assassination. The more quickly law enforcement officials could identify an assassin—even if they were not completely certain of his guilt—the more quickly they would quiet the public's fears of a conspiracy.

Hoover and the FBI also could have wanted to close the case quickly to hide the fact that it had pre-assassination contact with Oswald. Any ties to him would have embarrassed the Bureau. But there is still another, darker possibility: that FBI agents participated in a conspiracy to kill Kennedy. Hoover's eagerness to convict Oswald would stem then from a desire to preserve the Bureau's reputation.

Since the assassination, the FBI has done little to satisfy public curiosity about its role. Just as the CIA has refused to turn over storehouses of vital information, so has the FBI refused to release many of its own key assassination files. The available evidence does not strongly suggest direct FBI participation. But that only leads researchers to wonder what the FBI's *un*available files do suggest. When adding up all the possible FBI roles, researchers can reach only the familiar conclusion that there is no definite conclusion.

The Secret Service: The President's Personal Guard

Day to day, no organization works closer to a U.S. president than the Secret Service. As an intelligence organization, the only secret information it gathers involves the president; its primary job is to protect the president's personal safety. Secret Service agents are responsible, for instance, for ensuring the president's safety while he is traveling. It is common for them to provide almost constant protection for a president. They accompany chief executives almost

"I've got to insist that it was pure coincidence—that I will be strongly emphatic about. . . . I have no control over what the CIA did or did not do down in Mexico."

Former CIA employee William Gaudet explaining how his name appeared next to Oswald's on a list of Mexican entry papers, *Conspiracy.*

"After a few hours with William Gaudet, a reporter comes away . . . with an impression of a man who knows more . . . than he dares to discuss on the record."

Author Anthony Summers, *Conspiracy.*

wherever they go.

The official records show that the Secret Service performed this protective role for President Kennedy on his fateful trip to Dallas. There are odd, unexplained discrepancies, though, that suggest a different role for some Secret Service agents that day. In fact, some of the men who were sworn to protect Kennedy might have helped assure his death.

One source of suspicion was the unexplained appearance of Secret Service personnel in Dealey Plaza immediately after the assassination. Before the rifle shots, Secret Service agents were riding in various cars in the motorcade. Agent William Greer was driving Kennedy's limousine. Agent Roy Kellerman rode in the car's front passenger seat. Agent Clinton Hill rode on the driver's-side running board of the limousine behind Kennedy's. Other agents rode in other cars in

Taking a break from testifying before the House Assassinations Committee are the three Secret Service agents who were with Kennedy the day he was killed. On the left is Clinton Hill who rode in the car following the president. Roy Kellerman, in the middle, rode in the right front seat of the president's car and William Greer, right, drove the president's limousine.

This view of the School Book Depository was taken looking up Elm Street. To the left, near the stairs and the street sign, is the grassy knoll where police officer Joe Smith thought he would find the assassin.

the motorcade. According to official Secret Service records, all agents in Dallas that day accompanied Kennedy to Parkland Hospital immediately after the shooting.

A number of witnesses, though, offer testimony that directly contradicts the official record. Many people reported that they spoke to Secret Service agents in Dealey Plaza just after the assassination. After the final shot rang out, Dallas policeman Joe Marshall Smith raced behind the grassy knoll north of Elm Street. Smith got there so soon that he expected to see the fleeing assassin. He did smell gunpowder behind the row of trees, but all he saw was a quiet parking lot—and a man who identified himself as a Secret Service agent. According to official records, this man could not possibly have been a Secret Service agent. No one has ever identified him. Was he

This artist's drawing was one of the Warren Commission exhibits which was used because the autopsy photos were locked away. The drawing, based on autopsy details, shows the bullet entering at the base of the neck and exiting at the throat. But critics say the bullet entered from the front.

a Secret Service agent, as he claimed? Or was he carrying false identification so he could confuse the first wave of investigators? If his Secret Service papers were false, why was he hiding his identity? Could he have been the assassin? Or could he have been helping the real assassin escape?

One assassination researcher, David S. Lifton, theorizes that Secret Service personnel altered the appearance of Kennedy's wounds after the assassination. Lifton bases his conclusion on a meticulous comparison of the Dallas doctors' and the U.S. Navy doctors' descriptions of Kennedy's wounds. The Dallas doctors first saw Kennedy at 12:38 that Friday afternoon, only eight minutes after the assassination. They concluded that all the shooting had come from in front of and to the right of Kennedy. They described what looked like an entrance wound in Kennedy's throat, another entrance wound in his right temple, and a gaping exit wound at the back of his skull that measured thirty-five square centimeters. No Dallas doctor reported any entrance wound in Kennedy's neck or back or at the base of his skull. If the Dallas doctors were right, a gunman could have been stationed on the grassy knoll.

Secret Service Stops Autopsy

The Parkland Hospital doctors wanted to perform an autopsy in Dallas. Secret Service agents vehemently opposed them. They said that only official government doctors could make the final determinations about Kennedy's death. The Secret Service won. Under its supervision, Kennedy's body was flown to the U.S. Naval Medical Hospital in Bethesda, Maryland. The official autopsy began there more than six-and-a-half hours after the assassination.

The descriptions of Kennedy's wounds that emerged from the official autopsy were strikingly different from the original descriptions in Dallas. According to the official autopsy report, the exit wound in Kennedy's skull had grown. In Dallas, it measured thirty-five square centimeters. At the official autopsy, the exit wound in Kennedy's skull measured 170 square centimeters—almost five times larger than it had been just minutes after the assassination. The exit wound on Kennedy's skull now was so large that it included his right temple. Naval medical doctors also recorded entrance wounds at the back of Kennedy's shoulder and at the base of his skull. The autopsy findings indicated that a gunman had fired on Kennedy from behind.

How did the wounds change? Lifton concludes that someone must have altered the body. The Secret Service oversaw the transportation of the body from Dallas to Maryland. This was the interval during which Lifton thinks the appearance of the president's

Dr. Michael Baden who was chief medical examiner of New York City points to an illustration showing the bullet path through Kennedy's head. Dr. Baden was giving expert testimony for the House Committee.

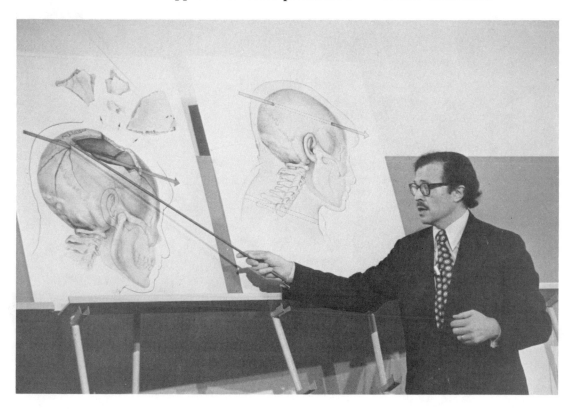

wounds changed. According to Lifton, the "data" of Kennedy's body was changed so that it looked like it had been shot from behind rather than from the front and to the right. In his theory, then, the real assassin fired from the grassy knoll; it is possible that no shots were fired from the Texas School Book Depository behind the president. If Lifton is right, Secret Service agents played a powerful role in shaping the way recent American history is understood. If no assassin fired from behind Kennedy, then whoever might have changed the appearance of the wounds literally *rewrote* history to agree with a false explanation of the assassination.

Jacqueline Kennedy and Robert Kennedy accompany the president's body to Bethesda Naval Hospital for the autopsy. If Secret Service agents altered the wounds, they had to do it before the body reached Washington.

Standard Form 503
Revised August 1954
Promulgated
By Bureau of the Budget
Circular A—32 (Rev.)

Commission Exhibit No. 387

| CLINICAL RECORD | AUTOPSY PROTOCOL A63-272 (JJH:ec) |

DATE AND HOUR DIED
22 November 1963 1300(CST) P.M.

DATE AND HOUR AUTOPSY PERFORMED
22 November 1963 2000(EST) M.

CHECK ONE
FULL AUTOPSY | HEAD ONLY | TRUNK ONLY

PROSECTOR (497831)
CDR J. J. HUMES, MC, USN

ASSISTANT (435378)
CDR "J" THORNTON BOSWELL, MC, USN   X
LCOL PIERRE A. FINCK, MC, USA (04 043 322)

CLINICAL DIAGNOSES (including operations)

Ht. - 72½ inches
Wt. - 170 pounds
Eyes - blue
Hair - Reddish brown

PATHOLOGICAL DIAGNOSES

CAUSE OF DEATH: Gunshot wound, head.

APPROVED—SIGNATURE
J. J. HUMES, CDR, MC, USN

MILITARY ORGANIZATION
PRESIDENT, UNITED STATES | AGE 46 | SEX Ma

PATIENT'S IDENTIFICATION
KENNEDY, JOHN F.
NAVAL MEDICAL SCHOOL

PATHOLOGICAL EXAMINATION REPORT   A63-272   Page 2

CLINICAL SUMMARY: According to available information the
deceased, President John F. Kennedy,
was riding in an open car in a motorcade during an official visit to Dallas, Texas
on 22 November 1963. The President was sitting in the right rear seat with Mrs.
Kennedy seated on the same seat to his left. Sitting directly in front of the
President was Governor John B. Connolly of Texas and directly in front of Mrs. Kennedy
sat Mrs. Connolly. The vehicle was moving at a slow rate of speed down an incline
into an underpass that leads to a freeway route to the Dallas Trade Mart wherethe
President was to deliver an address.

                                        Three shots were heard and the President
fell forward bleeding from the head. (Governor Connolly was seriously wounded by the
same gunfire.) According to newspaper reports ("Washington Post" November 23, 1963)
Bob Jackson, a Dallas "Times Herald"Photographer, said he looked around as he heard
the shots and saw a rifle barrel disappearing into a window on an upper floor of the
nearby Texas School Book Depository Building.

                                        Shortly following the wounding of the two
men the car was driven to Parkland Hospital in Dallas. In the emergency room of that
hospital the President was attended by Dr. Malcolm Perry. Telephone communication with
Dr. Perry on November 23, 1963 develops the following information relative to the ob-
servations made by Dr. Perry and procedures performed there prior to death.

                                        Dr. Perry noted the massive wound of the
head and a second much smaller wound of the low anterior neck in approximately the
midline. A tracheostomy was performed by extending the latter wound. At this point
bloody air was noted bubbling from the wound and an injury to the right lateral wall
of the trachea was observed. Incisions were made in the upper anterior chest wall
bilaterally to combat possible subcutaneous emphysema. Intravenous infusions of blood
and saline were begun and oxygen was administered. Despite these measures cardiac
arrest occurred and closed chest cardiac massage failed to re-establish cardiac action.
The President was pronounced dead approximately thirty to forty minutes after receiving
his wounds.

                                        The remains were transported via the
Presidential plane to Washington, D.C. and subsequently to the Naval Medical School,
National Naval Medical Center, Bethesda, Maryland for postmortem examination.

GENERAL DESCRIPTION OF BODY: The body is that of a muscular, well-
                                        developed and well nourished adult Caucasian
male measuring 72½ inches and weighing approximately 170 pounds. There is beginning
rigor mortis, minimal dependent livor mortis of the dorsum, and early algor mortis. The
hair is reddish brown and abundant, the eyes are blue, the right pupil measuring 8 mm.
in diameter, the left 4 mm. There is edema and ecchymosis of the inner canthus region
of the left eyelid measuring approximately 1.5 cm. in greatest diameter. There is edema
and ecchymosis diffusely over the right supra-orbital ridge with abnormal mobility of
the underlying bone. (The remainder of the scalp will be described with the skull.)

Crowds of people stand outside the emergency entrance of Parkland Hospital waiting for word of the president's condition.

Such a theory conveniently explains the apparent changes in Kennedy's wounds. In a roundabout way, it might even explain the presence of the fake Secret Service agent in the parking lot behind the grassy knoll. But is it true? Is it possible that the Dallas doctors, in their desperate attempt to save Kennedy's life, simply did not notice wounds on his back? Jean Davison, in her book *Oswald's Game*, calls Lifton's entire theory "preposterous." Which side is more believable? If there was a conspiracy, were Secret Service agents some of the co-conspirators? Or were they innocent of any crime?

As the other theories do, Lifton's points out serious flaws in the evidence and asks important questions. It offers a plausible explanation for some of the events surrounding John Kennedy's assassination. But does this mean that the theory is necessarily true? Other theories offer other explanations; and they, too, are based on logical conclusions from the available evidence. To a degree, all of them ''make sense''— but they cannot all be completely correct. Which one offers the best explanation? Which one is most correct? Which one the least?

An objective reader still cannot answer such questions with complete certainty. This comes as no surprise to seasoned students of the assassination. In this investigation, it is the solid evidence that causes surprise and disbelief. In John F. Kennedy's assassination, mysteries and unsolved riddles are the commonplace.

Five

An Enduring Mystery

Who killed John F. Kennedy?

Lee Harvey Oswald? A professional Mafia assassin? A team of "renegade" U.S. intelligence operatives? Some combination of the three?

Was the assassination a freak accident caused by one lone, deranged individual or a carefully plotted conspiracy? That question still lies at the heart of the assassination debate. The Dallas police, the FBI, and the Warren Commission stated the case for a lone assassin early in the investigation. In the years since then, however, contradictory evidence has continued to surface and strengthen the argument in favor of a conspiracy.

Evidence has mounted, for instance, that at least one Oswald impostor was in circulation in the South before the assassination. According to the official theory, Oswald was in Mexico City between September 25 and October 1, 1963. In one instance which suggests an Oswald impersonator, however, Silvia Odio, an exiled Cuban woman who lived in Dallas, reported that Oswald had stood on her front porch on either September 26 or 27 that year. According to her, three men—two Cubans and an American—came to

During a re-creation of the assassination, this picture was taken through a telescopic gun sight from the window of the School Book Depository from which the fatal shots were fired. The car was positioned at the same place on Elm Street where the president's car was when he was shot. This is what the assassin would have seen when he pulled the trigger.

"A reasonable interpretation [of the visit] is that the mysterious 'Leopoldo'—an anti-Castro plotter—was deliberately using the name of the real Oswald to set him up as the fall guy."

Author Anthony Summers, *Conspiracy.*

"When Mrs. Odio saw Lee Harvey Oswald on television after his arrest, she recognized him immediately as 'Leon Oswald.' Her sister, Annie Laurie Odio, who had seen the three visitors briefly, independently recognized Oswald."

Author Sylvia Meagher, *Accessories After the Fact.*

her house, uninvited and unannounced, at about nine in the evening. The larger of the two Cubans spoke for his companions. He introduced the shy, quiet American as "Leon Oswald." The larger Cuban identified himself as a friend of Odio's father, whom Castro supporters had jailed in Cuba. The larger Cuban wanted Odio to help the anti-Castro cause.

That visit shook Silvia Odio so much that she contacted her father in Cuba. Based on her descriptions, he did not recognize either of the two Cubans. The day after the visit, Silvia Odio received a telephone call from a man who identified himself as one of the Cubans. He asked her what she thought of "Leon" Oswald. He said that Oswald was "kind of nuts" and that he was inclined to kill President Kennedy.

Did Anti-Castro Rebels Frame Oswald?

Less than two months later, after the assassination, Silvia Odio recognized the face of Lee Harvey Oswald immediately. She told her story to the Warren Commission. The story she told disagreed with the official theory. It even suggested that still another group, anti-Castro extremists, could have conspired against both Kennedy and Oswald in the fall of 1963. Before the FBI ended its investigation of Odio's story, the Warren Commission dismissed it. On the basis of other evidence, it decided "that Lee Harvey Oswald was not at Mrs. Odio's apartment in September 1963." In 1978, the House Select Committee on Assassinations did not dismiss her story. The committee found Silvia Odio's odd tale both credible and significant.

How many Oswalds were there? How was Oswald in Dallas and Mexico City at the same time? If he was in Dallas, why was he with men whose political views apparently were opposite of his own? Why did one of them tell Silvia Odio that Oswald was a potential assassin? Is it possible that a group of anti-Castro extremists used Oswald as *its* "patsy" in the assassination?

More evidence than this has accumulated in favor of a conspiracy theory. Other people besides Oswald with links to the assassination have died unnatural, unexplained deaths since November 1963. On February 17, 1967, New Orleans District Attorney Jim Garrison opened the first public legal inquiry in which suspects would be brought to trial for conspiring to kill John Kennedy. Garrison's first suspect was David Ferrie. Five days after Garrison started his proceedings, police found Ferrie's nude body in his New Orleans apartment. What appeared to be a suicide note was also at the scene. The entire note, including Ferrie's name, was typed. Could someone else have typed

Three members of the Warren Commission visit the School Book Depository as part of their investigation: Senators John Cooper (left), Richard Russell (center), and Hale Boggs (right). The members of the Warren Commission quickly decided to ignore Silvia Odio's story about Lee Harvey Oswald.

New Orleans District Attorney Jim Garrison opened an investigation of the assassination in 1967. Garrison's chief suspect was David Ferrie.

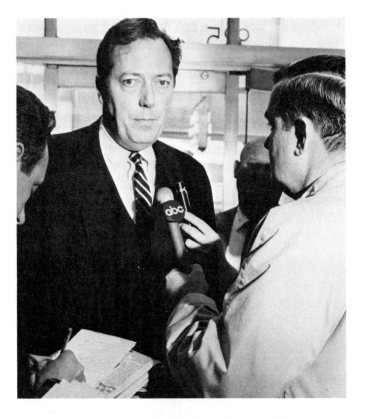

Ferrie's name as a safeguard against making a poor forgery? Was Ferrie's death a suicide or a carefully veiled murder that kept him from testifying about the assassination?

Ferrie spoke with a reporter only hours before his death. One subject they discussed was Jimmy Hoffa and the Teamsters Union. Did Ferrie, who worked for Carlos Marcello, know too much about Hoffa and his acquaintances? There is another substantial reason to speculate about the cause of Ferrie's death. On the same day that Ferrie died, Ferrie's close acquaintance, anti-Castro exile Eladio del Valle, was brutally murdered. Del Valle was also a reported associate of Santos Trafficante. District Attorney Garrison wanted to question del Valle, too, about the assassination. But before he could question him, the Cuban's body was found in a Miami parking lot. He had been shot once at point-blank range in the heart. In addition, his skull had been split open, probably with an axe.

Mysterious Deaths and Lost Evidence

Key witnesses also have died, often unnaturally. Bill Hunter was a reporter who searched Ruby's apartment only hours after Ruby shot Oswald. Hunter died of a gunshot wound in April 1964. Jim Koethe was a reporter who assisted Hunter. Koethe died five months later, in September 1964, from a karate chop to the neck. William Whaley was the Dallas taxi-driver who drove Oswald to his boardinghouse after the assassination. Whaley died in a motor vehicle accident in December 1965. Lee Bowers was a railroad worker who saw men acting suspiciously behind the grassy knoll before and after the assassination. Bowers died in a motor vehicle accident in August 1966. James Worrell Jr., witnessed a man fleeing the Texas School Book Depository just seconds after the shooting. Worrell died in a motor vehicle accident in November 1966. Over the years, even more witnesses have died mysteriously before their time. At one point, more than two-thirds of the deaths of assassination witnesses resulted from unnatural causes. Were their deaths only accidents, results of wild coincidence? Or does such a high death rate for such a small population indicate that they died because someone wanted them to die?

Crucial physical evidence has steadily vanished over the years, too. Sometime between April 1965 and October 1966, for instance, the most important piece of evidence in the case—John Kennedy's brain—disappeared while under U.S. government security. In addition, the catalogue of original autopsy photos has shrunk one key photo at a time. Investigative records—like Oswald's military intelligence files and Ferrie's FBI files—have been destroyed, presumably as a part of routine bureaucratic procedures. But can we attribute the loss or destruction of such vital

"The coroner of New Orleans, Dr. Nicholas Chetta, said Ferrie died of a ruptured blood vessel in his brain."

Journalist Peter Noyes, *Legacy of Doubt*.

"On February 22, 1967, David Ferrie was found dead at home. The coroner's ruling said 'natural causes,' but the death caused great speculation. Ferrie left behind two ambiguous notes. They suggested suicide, but the text and signature, in each note, was typed."

Author Anthony Summers, *Conspiracy*.

The riderless horse, whose stirrups hold boots in reverse to mark its rider's death, stands next to the caisson which will carry the president's casket from the U.S. Capitol where he had lain in state to St. Matthew's Cathedral, and then to Arlington National Cemetery.

evidence to "routine" procedures or accident? Or is it part of an ongoing operation designed to hide the identities of the real assassin and any possible conspirators?

Perhaps we can best answer those questions by remembering the questions with which we began: Who killed John F. Kennedy, and why? Even today, to that question and all the questions that follow from it, the surest answer is that John F. Kennedy's assassination is an enduring mystery that remains unsolved.

For Further Exploration

Jim Bishop, *The Day Kennedy Was Shot*. New York: Funk & Wagnalls, 1968.

Michael Canfield and Alan J. Weberman, *Coup d'Etat in America: The CIA and the Assassination of John F. Kennedy*. New York: The Third Press, 1975.

Jean Davison, *Oswald's Game*. New York: W. W. Norton, 1983.

David Gates, et al., "The Kennedy Conundrum: Still Too Many Questions—Still Too Many Answers," *Newsweek*, November 28, 1988.

Henry Hurt, *Reasonable Doubt: An Investigation into the Assassination of John F. Kennedy*. New York: Holt, Rinehart and Winston, 1985.

David S. Lifton, *Best Evidence: Disguise and Deception in the Assassination of John F. Kennedy*. New York: Macmillan, 1980.

William Manchester, *The Death of a President, November 20-November 25, 1963*. New York: Harper & Row, 1967.

Sylvia Meagher, *Accessories After the Fact: The Warren Commission, the Authorities and the Report*. Indianapolis: Bobbs-Merrill, 1967.

George O'Toole, *The Assassination Tapes: An Electronic Probe into the Murder of John F. Kennedy and the Dallas Cover-up*. New York: Penthouse Press, 1975.

David E. Scheim, *Contract on America: The Mafia Murders of John and Robert Kennedy*. Silver Spring, MD: Argyle Press, 1983.

Anthony Summers, *Conspiracy*. New York: McGraw-Hill, 1980.

Josiah Thompson, *Six Seconds in Dallas: A Micro-Study of the Kennedy Assassination*. New York: Bernard Geis Associates, 1967.

United Press International and *American Heritage* magazine, *Four Days*. New York: American Heritage Publishing, 1964.

U.S. House of Representatives Select Committee on Assassinations, *Report of the Select Committee on Assassinations: Findings and Recommendations*. 95th Congress, 2nd Session. House Report No. 95-1828, part 2.

U.S. President's Commission on the Assassination of John F. Kennedy, *Investigation of the Assassination of President John F. Kennedy: Hearings and Exhibits*. 26 vols. Washington, DC: U.S. Government Printing Office, 1964.

U.S. President's Commission on the Assassination of John F. Kennedy, *Report of the President's Commission on the Assassination of President John F. Kennedy*. Washington, DC: U.S. Government Printing Office, 1964.

Index

Picture Credits

The National Archives, 32, 70, 72, 82, 95
In the John F. Kennedy Library, Photo No. USA Signal Corps SC 578830, 10
Library of Congress, 11, 12, 15, 26, 29, 55, 58, 86, 87, 88
AP/Wide World Photos, 14T, 16, 17, 19, 20, 22, 23, 25, 30, 31, 33, 35, 36, 39, 43, 44, 47, 48, 54, 56, 57, 61, 68, 69, 71,
    75, 78, 79, 83, 90, 91, 92, 104
Mary Ahrndt, 14B, 21
UPI/Bettmann Newsphotos, 9, 28, 37, 42, 51, 53, 59, 62, 64, 67, 77, 80, 81, 85, 93, 94, 96, 99, 101, 102
Courtesy Lyndon B. Johnson Library, 46

About the Author

Jeffrey Waggoner was born and raised in Palestine, Illinois. After high school, he attended Southern Illinois University in Carbondale, Illinois, where he earned a B.S. in Forestry and an M.A. in English. Since completing his formal studies, Jeffrey has moved to central Wisconsin. A writer by trade, he has written direct mail pieces, ads, press releases, and other promotional assignments.

Jeffrey's main non-writing interests are breeding field trial calibre Labrador retrievers, studying astronomy, and organic gardening.

Some of Jeffrey's earliest memories involve John F. Kennedy's assassination; he was only three-and-a-half years old at the time. His memories of that weekend led him to research and write this book.